PREFACE

I BEGAN TO write late in retirement as part of a carefully planned regime which included healthy eating, excercise and other invigorating pursuits I thought appropriate and necessary, to keep my head above the wall of incomprehension that my atrophied brain insidiously builds around me.

The world as I see it, is a defunct part of a nobody knows what for, or why, *Thingy-Me-Bob*. Evicted from the the fringe of its primary purpose. A useless, fermenting, rotting, clinker, wobbling around the firmament, being naturally disposed of in violent competition by a parasitical combination of hostile fauna and flora. In nature's reliable "maggots on a dead dog" way. All this goes on unnoticed as we grope through the carnage that is life toward each our inevitable unhappy ending. If you have not quite made your mind up whether I'm a pessimist or prophet ... *read on*. (There are funny bits too!)

Rocket science has been around longer than you might think. Starting in new testament times – albeit in a primitive way – at the holiest period of the Christian calender. It was ingenious mathematical timing guaranteed that Jesus didn't ascend prematurely like a rocket on a stick, that Friday.
It was two thousand years later a plausable explanation for the ascention emerged when pensioners Tom and Tess decided to end it all in a way that was not as original as they thought...

TOM AND TESS'S BUDGET FLIGHT

Sat sitting in their quaint old fashioned
forties style front room
a ninety year old couple
contemplate impending doom.

We've dwelt contented in this house
for sixty years and more
most of them were happy
excepting three or four.

Gazing at the blazing fire
each smilingly recalls
frozen moments in old pictures
hung around familiar walls.

I've been thinking, said old Tom out loud
to his adoring spouse,
it's getting to the time
we can't maintain our little house.

I don't want to be a burden
and neither I think do you
so I've made a plan
for an easy way out
simultaneously for two.

You mean to enact a suicide pact
she responded with mounting concern.
There's a growing trend t'ward multiple end
for them lonely...with nowhere to turn.

But what about God's holy teachings
regarding... do it yourself demise?
They say he gets very angry
not invited, to supervise.

You don't have to worry my darling
we'll accomplish the whole thing with ease
on larger than average helpings
of cabbage and marrow fat peas.

Neighbours worried, enquire to each
have you seen old Tom and Tess?
Constable breaks door down
the quicker to access.

Staggers back in horror
at the smell and rasping sounds
from a pair of bloated corpses
levitating off the ground.

After the embalming
the mortician and his missis
completed the job on Tom and Tess
plugging up... their orifices.

Friends in pews at the Crematorium
unaware of swelling methane
in Tess and Tom's dead tums
were suddenly sent reeling
when both as one, burst coffin lids
and shot up to the ceiling.
Straight through a stained glass fanlight
like rockets toward Heaven –
scared the shit from all aboard
a passing seven four seven.

Down at the Crematorium
the Vicar's looking pleased
even though it looks as though
he'll not get any fees.
For as Tom and Tess leave scorch marks
hurtling through the trees
he sits broadly smiling,
in the artificial breeze.

Now certain of what tucker
was served at the last supper,
from which Jesus heartily ate,
and shared with his Desciples
off a larger than average plate
gets in touch with his local Bishop
on his mobile phone by text
excitedly, sends a thesis
of what likely happened next.

Whilst Peter and Paul,
proposed a world tour
eating soup of the day and cheese
Jesus, planning an exit
that would bring them to their knees,
scoffed a bigger than average helping
of cabbage and marrowfat peas.

So if you want to spike convention
and care to emulate
choose the luxury, or alternate
cheap affordable rate.

Number One's the best of produce
organic and sure to please.
Or the TESCO everyday blast off
supercharged with their own branded peas.

The committee on global warming I hear
are now overwhelmingly keen,
to subsidise funeral expenses
on condition, we all go green.

Burial grounds redundant
the future resting place
is spinning round the milky way,
on the outer edge of space.

Buy yourself a telescope
and on Sunday afternoon
catch a glimpse of Gran and Grandpa
orbiting the moon.

There's a small blue plaque
on that quaint little house
dedicated to Tom and his loving old spouse
I mustn't forget to mention.
Donated by Richard Dawkins
for busting the myth of ascension.

AT LAST I KNOW NOW WHERE I'M @

I'm just like any other old person wondering where all the time went sat here slowing down, recapitulating events till the finishing post comes into view.

Thinking of things like you do
why am I me why are you, you?
Frogs, insects, them in the zoo
what are we all put down here to do?

Conceived from cuddles and kisses
That's wonderful, that's fine,
it's unfortunate from the outset though
We're in permanent decline.

Been on this earth a long time now
eighty years, and plenty
soon I'll be moving I don't know where?
My bed, left cold, and empty
I've written many theories
as to why, and what life's for,
gave up, without an answer
don't care much any more.

Quite spritely for my age it's said
often out to dine
An avid listener to Radio Four
Brew beer, and ferment wine

Have had a go at making jam
strawberry, raspberry, plum
can climb up steps to decorate
still able to wipe me bum!

I'm way off the elusive answer
for a reason to exist
have lost my curiosity now
for what humanity persists.
After stoic competition
in the uphill human race
The explanation as to,
"what's it about?"
has been staring me in the face

Mental pictures of my future
were obscured by irrational fears
when the job interviewer asked me
where I'd be in fifty years.
Disciplined since in different regimes
time measured by ticking clocks
today if asked the same question
I'd with certainty say: in a box.

Thumbing through those bygone days
signposted
ups and downs,
the periods of happiness
outnumber many frowns.
While fellow peers forge second careers

I live in a sheltered flat,
eat a healthy diet
pass time doing this and that
I'm certainly not wealthy,
and there's things I can't afford
but I've stumbled across the meaning of life
like him, that found the lost chord.

My reward for that eighty year struggle
over life's symbolic miles,
is two gorgeous great granddaughters.
Heart melting innocent smiles.

IT HAD TO BE SAID SOONER OR LATER

There comes a time writing poetry when one begins to seriously doubt its quality after having published a couple to little or no reaction. I have noticed though that humorous poetry generally is not taken very seriously. Daft as they might be, many funny poems convey a light hearted wisdom of their own that to me equals the more traditionally accepted bias favoured soberly expressed, rhymed or otherwise profundity.

When I write a poem, or anything come to that
is it everyday banality bereft of imaginallity?
Sent a sample to the printer for a warts and all critique
a cry for help, a whimpering yelp, a last attempt to seek
is my work pathetic crap or in any way unique?
Will he recommend anything like
having a go at open mic?
Save my cash and publish
Give it up completely,
accept it's f..kin rubbish

He responded:
Poems are like seaside rock, that each successive bite
brings back a sweet reminder of weekends, boozy nights
clanking up to Clevelys, in trams on silver lines
youthful indiscretions, drinking cider, quaffing wines
strolls along the sea front, eating burgers, holding hands
bucket and spade, warm lemonade,
tiddly om pom bands.

Memories come flooding back, as you nibble lick and chew it
what do you see to the very last bite?
Nostalgia running through it

Your work, he carried on, is of a similar confection
but without the rich ingredients,
to be worthwhile contemplation;
the audio was dreadful, so amateur and nasal –
Well, you did ask for a warts and all, no holds barred appraisal.

My overall opinion whilst avoiding to offend
give up now, don't waste your time
I strongly recommend
try collecting beer mats
give up poetry my friend.

The message I see conveyed to me,
and experts would agree
yours too identifies with a stick of rock,
but with juvernility:
limp, soppy, insipid
childish, unable to send
messages of any kind
inspire the spirits ascend

Your total lack of talent
can be attributed I think
to being one from a long line of pillocks,
thick as a Belfast sink.

Having chewed the length of *your* candy
metaphorically I see,
endorsed in raspberry flavour
worst *EVER* poet… that's me.

SMILES

It's hard enough to find a job these days, but even worse if you're born with a very sensitive laughing gene, that could almost be described as a disability. Alright at parties, but embarassing round Granddad's death bed. Having a good sense of humour is ok in its place but first you need to know which situations are appropriate.

I'm a unique inhabitant of this earth
with predisposed uncontrollable mirth
when placed in the cot
number four in the litter
an astonished Nurse exclaimed:
"Could've sworn, I heard a titter"

Mother lying on the bed
throbbing hips aching head
grimacing at stretch marks
over sore lactating tit, says
"I'm really glad, *some* bugger's
seen the funny side of it!"

Growing up in this large brood
and always in a happy mood
got more slaps than the other three
for laughing when I shouldn't be
social services got involved.

Making a twenty-four hour graph
of me smiling, chuckling, giggling,
between side splitting belly laughs
the occupational therapist, looked thoughtfully then said:
"I find this case most puzzling, he's difficult to assess
having never seen a case like this
I reservedly acquiesce
to your having a few more quid a week,
apply to the DSS."

Having never heard of an illness as such
a condition brought on through laughing too much
officials conferring took hours to agree
that: "Until the time we can or will,
discover a cure, maybe a pill,
to make your son more miserable,
we're willing to go those extra miles
and award him benefits, for involuntary smiles.

Meanwhile
find him a job,
hard manual action,
where laughing won't be
too big a distraction."

Despairing of finding a job location
I stumbled upon my true vocation
laughing at comedians, in a home
suffering severe 'unfunny syndrome'

I was paid to grin and giggle
at unbelieveably bad jokes
split my sides at conunderums
till I was fit to choke,
peals of laughter, permanent chuckle,
nonstop crudities near the knuckle
night time rich with double entendres
tales of french knickers, ladies' suspenders
learner drivers, the highway code
and why the chicken crossed the road.

Now retired, on my own
memories return of that rehab home
I count amongst my circle of friends
hundreds of unfunny comedians.

Now! what of that famous leghorn
performing its road crossing tricks.
Just a built-in genetical mission
"he was after pulling chicks"

Being realistic as we no doubt should
he ended up like most chickens would
kentucky deep fried, finger lickin' good,
deep down suppose, I don't really care
the times he crossed that thoroughfare
I fall about, laughing still
the reasons are uncountable.

I hear the last time he crossed the road
was to see a hard core movie
when the lights went down he gave a frown
got very upset and deluded
instead of the advertised,
FLOCK AROUND THE COCK,
it was BATTERIES NOT INCLUDED.

REFLECTIONS ON MAN'S FINAL JOURNEY

Celibate Priests, Fundamentalist Imams,
eagerly preach their delusive plans
Protestant Vicars and Methodist lays,
give it out in gentler ways,
to simple folk in hallowed halls
with pointy tops, round minarets,
brass artefacts, smooth marble steps.

The use of loud hailers and noisy bells
call the faithful to worship and God to please
devotions observed on bended knees,
while venerable leaders in vigorous dispute
offer paths to Heaven by differing route
on varying surfaces stony or smooth,
stony it seems the most 'with it' groove.

Walk up, walk up, walk up this way,
walk up for sentence on judgement day,
when your average decent Joe and Jane
hoping years of piety were not in vain,
smile as they anticipate
the joy, the peace, tranquillity,
beyond that pearly gate.

The suicide bomber with quickening pace
savours pleasures awaiting, Heaven within,
can't wait to ravage, his first virgin,
anxious, impatient, full of self important worth.

Hope she's not so ugly
as his last act on Earth.

Now the time has come to be profound
'cause when we're dead and in the ground,
having lost all emotion and concupiscence
perform the same task in unison,
decaying slowly without strife,
compulsory cohesion,
preposterous in life.

THE INSIDIOUS PROCESS OF DECAY

From being young, having seen, been told
I've had this fear of growing old
a joint creaking, pill taking, medicinal hell
encompassed in an atmospheric,
geriatric smell.

But now I've gotten old myself
no hair, few teeth fell off the shelf
in reasonable health though poor in wealth
I'm not depressed, ill or sad
this being old "is not so bad"
I'm feeling fit and keeping well
recite bad poems at the Ring O' Bell
no inhibitions confident bolder
don't suffer (I think) old people odour.

Best of my day has got to be
after dark when it's time for tea
smug warm wanting for nowt
pile food on the plate, proceed to pig out
a large glass of wine then two then many
find the remote, switch on the telly

Antiques Roadshow, Clarkson's top gears
Ant and Dec, The Three Musketeers
dash from the bathroom after a pee
don't want to miss what's next on TV
but the drink kicks in it's not to be
collapse flat out stretched on the settee

Three in the morning wake and rally
missed the end of Downton Abbey
stomach rumbles need food to ingest
snack on dried gravy peeled off 'f me chest
discard the underpants socks and vest
lay weary head on flat pillow to rest.

Vibrating snores ripple stubbled cheek
good job I drink only twice a week
content as a babe asleep in its cot
one happy wine stained old bundle of grott.
The whole place needs cleaning
losing the plot
couldn't care less, if I'm smelly or not.

WHAT'S IT ALL ABOUT?

In days of old, at the dawn of time
when life was microbes in primal slime
Mother Nature in contemplation
declared the start of repeat creation.

Varieties of life, will grow and mate
in a unique way to perpetuate
forms of life with various span
plus one special item, "intelligent man";
where worldly creatures, whatever stations,
will in death... enrich the Earth,
for future generations.

But Man with his growing self-esteem
couldn't bear to think, one's final sleep
would be one of decay on a compost heap.
Persuaded his fellows, to believe there's a place
a mythical Heaven somewhere in space.
Where spirits float for ever more
in states of moral grace.

Left over, redundant, the mortal coil,
is then dug deep into the waiting soil
with relevant prayers the kin to assure.
A bit over the top... for spreading manure.

So beware when Preachers promise
"eternal life, this better place"
sounds profound, but it's a hole in the ground
without any moral grace.
A tiny stinking empty space
twixt coffin lid and rotting face
absorbed in the earth, destined to bring
re-creation in future springs.

Mandatory death, with reluctant cooperation
is the final act of each generation
performed by everyone, in time
reverted back to 'primal slime'.
From preloved placentas, plugged deep in the soil
grows food for life's infinite toil.

What better way to contribute a lasting legacy of life
enriching and confirming another year's bountiful growth
through the remnants of plants and progeny
eternally passed on by the ultimate in physical pleasure?

CATTLE ARE SLAUGHTERED IN HUMANE MANNER

NOT SO HIM WHO CARRIES A BANNER

I make no apology for the blunt upsetting scenario in this piece and the cynicism portrayed, just dismiss it as the product of an overipe mind, unbalanced after a lifetime of ill-advised decision making, during which struggles between common sense and violent emotion, ended all too often in victory for the latter.
Anything can be made to sound morally acceptable, tempered by text comprised of carefully chosen words, from our over rich language.

I've thought and concluded, that since time began
in every generation, there's one wicked man,
unfeeling, no conscience, no sense of regret
no rules of engagement, just takes what he gets,
cunning by nature with multiple flaws,
sows poisoned seed on fallow minds that blossoms into wars
hypnotic skillful speeching, holding listeners mesmeric,
teases out our darker elements with clever rhetoric,
insanity ensues to approve expansive plans
for killing peaceful people off, in far flung foreign lands.

And when the battle is not progressing, as they think it ought to be,
it's upgraded to a 'Crusade' approved by God, to you and me.
This endorsed label of respectability,
guarantees a favourable bias, from here to Galilee.

Sermons from cathederals, by dignitaries of note,
identify mass genocide, to be the only hope,
for enduring peace much quicker.
They preach it's been OK'd by us, check with your local Vicar.

Destroying evil is a must but not quite sure why yet
we need a few more oil wells, pay the national debt.
Those heathens are protesting, it's aggression and unjust
we'll make a statement later on,
right now though can't be fussed.
Addressing the assembled troops, chest swelled out with pride.
Colonel shouts: *"It's in the bag,*
God is on our side".

Peace treaty signed, opponents slain,
exhausted warrior returned by train
picks up his trowel starts over again.
From the craft of murder to brickie reskilled
adjusts from destroying begins to rebuild,
a brighter future, brave new world
no more fighting ever again,
in a land fit for heroes our women and men.

Into the peace done paying the price,
for many the ultimate sacrifice.
Scars of conflict slowly healed,
been many a year since victory bells pealed.
Memories fade to opaque though unwilling,
of fallen comrades, enlistment shillings
blindings, cripplings, gassings, killings.

Governments come, Governments go,
today's incumbants too young, don't remember
the horrors recalled each year in November.
A century gone since World War One,
the war to end war they reckoned
but being unable, to forgive and forget,
a mere twenty years more saw the second.
International rumblings, inappropriate words,
could easily precipitate a catastrophic third.

And once again we'll take up arms encouraged by massed choirs,
lining up, stood face to face, in leafy abattoirs,
plasterers and plumbers wielding unfamiliar tools
comprise companies of trembling, terrified brainwashed fools.
Driven on to guns in knee deep cloying mud,
heaps of dead and wounded run rivulets of blood.
Platoon commander writes consoling parents of the dead
agonized screams of the dying, locked tight inside his head
of how their sons died bravely instant, without pain.
A lie to be repeated, again, again, and again

Munition barons profit from the cause of every death
returns from shares inflated with expended final breath.
As are the rats that feast upon,
their khaki clad largesse.

Why has God in all his wisdom, let things get ever worse?
Can't he alter old philosophy, modernise the verse?
I'd be a Christian Soldier and follow him with zeal

Don't hide behind the curtain, show everyone you're real.
He's been in charge since time began,
is he a frail, done, time worn man,
lost control of his burgeoning clan?
Folk leave the Church in droves because
they're convinced God's a fable,
a folklore *Wizard of Oz*.

Win back your spurs be a serious mentor,
encourage the brave conscientious objector,
give back the Earth to the the meek and the poor
cheeks to be kissed, not slapped any more;
encourage do-gooding with unpaid labour
make it mandatary loving thy neighbour –
In an ideal World with frontiers gone,
hearts and minds would be as one.
Poppy's significance, red beautiful flower
not to remind, of times cruel and dour.

LISTENERS' LETTERS

The BBC's mighty media machine can radicalise and lower the morals of those with the highest principals. How? you ask, I'll tell you! By stirring the basic instincts of vulnerable audiences, with cunningly scripted licentious plays on weekday afternoons.

In disgust I write this letter
to you at Radio Four
it's the afternoon plays and their context
couldn't sink to levels much lower.

My intense parochial piety
coupled with narrow minded morality
is incensed, dismayed, down-hearted
at the risque filth imparted
in this rapid downward trend,
I blame it on the new stuff
from the foul-mouthed younger end.

There was a time I could hardly wait
till Wednesday at two came round
listen to the Archers,
then with a cuppa settle down.

Tune in to your latest offering,
wholesome, clean, profound.
Actors, in iconic roles
morals impeccably sound.

They were decent upright with values,
entertaining, leisurely paced,

Now they're racey, salacious, and mostly
concern subjects below the waist.

The gratuitous graphic content
on an otherwise nice afternoon
embarrassed our visiting vicar
and my wife bumped her head in a swoon.

Proof of the impact, on her marginal health
you'll glean from the selfie, and note to yourself
from unbiassed circumspection.
My dearest lies trembling in the extension
perspiring profusely through pallid complexion.

The vicar's departed to visit more houses
hat held low down, conceals bulge in his trousers.
Your afternoon ratings have dwindled –
by three.
Shame on you, at the BBC.

Later, consulting his Bible, quotes from relevant paging,
calmed his unbridled ranting and raging,
dissuades him from being ashamed of his gender
glancing down at his resurrect member.

This message from God, through a radio play
reminds him that he, at the end of the day
can still get it up, and with guidance away.

Guilty feelings,
for his Radio Four reprimand,
overwhelmed by born again vigour
on taking himself in hand.

THE UNBEARABLE

This poem ventures into the sensitive area of political correctness regarding unfair favouritism afforded to a certain species.

What's so wonderful about Pandas,
why do people stand and stare
At what after all is only,
a black and white veggie bear?

A mysterious thing is a Panda
of which knowledge is vague and grey
but we do know because of its diet,
It shits, forty times, every day

Curious crowds are wide-eyed,
at their cuddlyness, "all agog"
not deliberately shy and elusive,
spend most of their time on the bog

If the World's population were Pandas
living on bamboo grass
and man the endangered species
would it ever come to pass?

I imagine myself loaned to China,
on the first of many trips
would Pandas turn up in their thousands
to watch ME, eat egg and chips?

A cry on behalf of all animals,
highlighting the disrespect
toward elephants, spiders and warthogs
from whales to the smallest insect
this bias in favour of Pandas
is politically incorrect

Agreeing with the protest
will be creatures of the night
screeching,
the public wouldn't love them so much
if they didn't have patches of white.

LOVE AT FIRST SIGHT

This is a story of true love between a man and his motor that sadly like most long term relationships with the passage of time, evolve into twilights of tedium.

Stood transfixed with staring eyes
in June two thousand and three.
admiring her fulsome sexy lines
latest gadgetry,

Glowing irridescent, in deep metalic blue
I was smitten from the start,
what a stylish beauty
be still my beating heart

Heard her engine running,
an almost silent purr
winking snide of a salesman whispers,
bet you'd like to be in her

Treat her soft and gentle
as you would a loving wife
then she'll willingly reciprecate,
with the best ride of your life

She's only got three cylinders,
performs like having four
Further salacious comments
leave me lusting even more
responds to the touch immediately
warmed up must 'ave her Coooah!

When it comes to upkeep,
she's a one in a million honey
will take you effortless, all the way
on micro amounts of money
Aquistition of a motor like this,
the perfect mechanical Venus
will replace your condition of low self esteem
with a large in the mind enhanced penis

We've been together many years
excursions now rare and few
it's only to be expected,
done thousands of miles from new

Difficult to prime, enthusiasm fake
exciting hours we used to share
she's grown to fear and dread.
Stalling constantly to put me off.
With an aching cylinder head.

NATURE'S EXTREMES

Just thought I'd throw this in.

The butterfly dances a ballet
over leaf, then blousy floret
a beautiful painted creature
from natures abundant chest
engaged in a brief but short lived,
urgent nectar quest.

Plant and insect seamlessly blend
to a sculpture, nature alone could intend.
links in life's chain perform earthly remits.
But imagine them minus,
the decorous bits.
You're left with gross creepy.
Six legged gits.

IS NO JOB SAFE?

Grim faced Mortician hurries on down
to the coffin makers conference, held in town,
agenda tucked, neath pinstriped arm
contains minutes of last meeting, plus items of alarm.

Medical breakthroughs prophesy longevity
life spans will exceed, two hundred and seventy
eyeballs, kidneys, hips, replacement knees
Cryonic-ally, kept in the deepest freeze
pale complexion? feeling livery?
order one now, free next day delivery
lungs in pairs, implanted hairs, shelves of beating hearts
buy them on the Internet,
put your purchase in the cart
a World without backache, no excuse to shirk
fit as a Butchers mongrel, no duvet days off work.

A cash strapped Chancellor pleads for us,
to be pennywise, frugal, and thrifty
with a promised drop in retirement age
down to one hundred and fifty

Worried delegates ill at ease
shout we can't have 'em living, as long as they please
infirmity banished, no deadly disease.
Chairman estimates through well practiced frown
the lack of cadavers will be profound
to incinerate, put in the ground,
but we'll meet the challenge, without delay

through drastic change, in a radical way.
assuring satisfaction.
Persuading doubters to accept ...
"death, is a must have attraction"

Secretary details what Committee has planned:
"A break to take,
a still alive wake,
at the EUTHANASIA GRAND
Escape a future that's all but immortal
Join the queue at our mock pearly portal
arrive in style, wear best suits and frocks
remember the good times, as well as the knocks
enjoy vintage wines, slurp Scotch on the rocks
sat up in your velvet lined, brass handled box"

Fed up having seen it, got the tee shirt, and all,
they'll be tempted in their thousands,
by our advert on the wall,
explaining how to snuff it,
fifty ways to end it all

A once in a lifetime offer
from infinity be freed
we take care of ALL your problems,
satisfaction guaranteed
sign up now, don't hesitate,
celebrate, drink wine
get help to throw the towel in,
avoid long term decline

A patriotic gesture on reaching ninety nine
is to think of Good Queen Bess's health
at this poignant time,
and save her from the irksome chore
She's never found much fun
of sending you a birthday card,
now you'll never reach the ton.

SHATTERED ASPIRATIONS BY THE UNKNOWN (*IT'S NOT ME!*) EX-POET

Browsed this site the other day
Write Out Loud its name,
publish your poems here, it said
to international acclaim.
Read a few on the net that day,
some were brilliant, some nowt to say
Some were happy, others sad
some were crappy, unbelievably bad.
some had rhyme, some without
didn't understand what most, were about

So I uploaded work on my account
of superior quality In huge amount
limerick, poem, monologue.
All condensed in an marathon blog,
the whole of me lifetimes catalogue.

Wearily stashed computer away
to await reviews, cum Saturday
snuggled under duvet,
for much needed relaxation
dreaming of tomorrows, unbridled adulation

DREAM SEQUENCE

Admirers in legions from Dumfries to Kent
generous with helpings of flattering testament,
describe my output among themselves
while queuing to empty, Waterstones shelves
minstrels sing, lyres a strumming,
compare me with, the second coming

Broadsheet headlines loudly scream.
" NEWFOUND WONDER BARD"
Ann Duffy says, "to top his stuff
I'll find it very hard"
column after column shouts,
"I'm so proud to be a Brit"
"loads of odes suit every mode
packed with sparkling wit"

"Poems for the working man
couldn't be outclassed"
"his natural sensitivity
not to be surpassed"
"failed to get my message in
the world wide web had crashed."
Critics on the Culture Show
mouth kudos unabashed.

"He's *SO* here, he's *SO* now"
how on earth he does it,
I simply don't know how!
...Julian waxing lyrical,
to a speechless Winston plowe,

Cynthia Buell Thomas gushes,
"where has this man been"
why so late to come upon on, the literary scene
this bright new star in write out loud
"master of the rhyme"
never thought I'd ever see,
a talent good as mine.

Julian and Winston, grudgingly agree
that verse for verse compared with me
their work is not as nice,
samey, predictable, forgetable
the genre of three blind mice.

they rue the day getting stuck in a rut
not taking their interests wider
slow to found a progressive school
"like"... Incy Wincy Spider
forced to admit alongside my work
theirs is vacuous, boring, banal,
Winston contemplates ending it all
in his Hebden Bridge stretch of canal.

Duffy, Gough, Armitage,
in mittens, finished, redundant,
seek winter warmth, burning unsold books,
thanking God,
stocks are vast and abundant.

BACK TO REALITY

Saturday night get booted up impatient to,
"bring it on"
anticipate lavish comments, for savouring one by one
eager to glean from ream after ream
what future beckons me
but instead of a toast, from an awe stricken host.
Get constructive abuse, for incorrect use,
of a fucking apostrophe.

CARING FOR LARGE PEOPLE NEEDS A HARD REGIME

I read this in The Lancet recently; it was an article highlighting the extra costs involved when someone dies as a result of being super obese. There are though, ways whereby some of this can be recouped with a little lateral thinking; this is to take advantage of the novelty aspect that someone deceased and grotesquely fat presents to a curious public.

Caring for the corpulent I find
the need for a program, of cruel to be kind
remind them constantly while you're there,
why they're so huge, wedged in a chair
grossly fat, a chin full of hair
an out of time attraction
for a nineteenth century fair

Fast food, slow food, food to take out
contribute enormously to dropsy and gout
MacDonald's, KFC, hot curry paste
all create that over hanging, eighty six inch waist
Cigarettes, alcohol, phlegm blocked chest
drooling down that freshly laundered
outsize hospital vest
a bed blocking, chewing machine,
in the cash starved, NHS
all wrapped up in a big top sized, M, and S. nightdress
Nurses brush potato crisps and crumbs from folds and creases
then finish off with fungus cream
to soften dried up faeces

Sister says you eat too much, chocolate sweets and nougat
glucose levels indicate, your body's two thirds sugar
blood pressure dangerous, and to me the obvious cause is
an abnormal greedy appetite to equal any horses
gobbling down big dinners, cream teas, and five pound
brunches
large enough to choke a pair,
of working, Suffolk Punches
greediness and indolence made you, this big fat blob
the only moving part *YOU* have
is that ever open gob

As a last resort on Doctors advice
It was decided to fit a gastric device
with disastrous results one evening
it snapped when devouring a custard pie
and the tea tray flew up to the ceiling

It's not just your welfare I hold dear
I've got this nagging inner fear
of costs incurred and need to be paid
to our local authority fire brigade
on certified demise
for lifting your carcass off the bed
by hoist and forklift truck
and making the window twice as wide
to stop it getting stuck.

It always attracts a morbid crowd
when news of this nature gets round

so we'll only have family flowers
and charge the rest a pound.
To see the flying fat lady
flutter to the ground

Rush what's left down the cryonics lab
preserved in a fridge on a marble slab
to await research in avoiding flab
before festering and putrid
thawed out again in a hundred years
when there's a cure, for fat... and stupid.

A BRIEF CHRONICLE OF LIFE IN SHELTERED ACCOMMODATION

I live in a place like this, it's a sort of scrapyard for old peeps.

Early risers wake and stir
unsure the day, the time, what year
birdsong greeting a fresh new dawning
accompanies sounds of retching and yawning
make a brew return to bed
Wardens check for the quick and the dead
this daily ritual, and early repast
for some old soul might be their last

Cliques in the lounge, members thin, and stout
suffering asthma diabetes and gout
tea and toast brought out the kitchen
effects a brief stay to the babble of bitching
tea cups emptied, pastries consumed
one or two Zimmer framed back to their rooms
those remaining relaxed replete
continue to gossip from favourite seat

Have you heard about her, in number three?
Daughter's researching the family tree
they'll find it easy says my old man
'cause her mum's been around since records began
and don't say I told you, but between me and thee I swear
those before her dropped out of a tree,
and that husband of hers if you see him outdoors
he's designed to perambulate about on all fours

Have you seen old Bert? Confined to his room
has regressed to eating food with a spoon
according to Betty he's well and happy
done the full circle back in a nappy

He was half asleep sat in a chair,
when asked who's Dave Cameron returned a blank stare
the Doctor assumed an authoritive air
and in layman's terms addressed everyone there
when a head gives up thinking, there's no cure for that!
but be happy to know, it can still wear a hat
this news wiped the smiles off the family's faces
the joke's proved prophetic, him in one of those places.

He's gone away now, a week since he went
and on clearing his flat they're anxiously bent
the quicker it's done, less time on it spent
they'll not have to pay an extra months rent.
Beloved armchair, chucked out, redundant
clears the way, for a next incumbent
cancelled papers, redirected mail
treasured possessions , on table top sale
day by day as mementos diminish
memories fade, flicker,then finish.

Our Sheltered Scheme plays a game in a league
demanding sharp mental endeavour it's difficult to pick a team, because at it, we're equally clever
In competition we swept the board, with a new World record setting
now we're Rochdale Boroughwide Champions.
At synchronized forgetting.

ANOTHER FINE MESS

I don't know whether you've noticed there's not much optimism in my stuff, well I've more bad news, here's another smile subduer.

Election over finished and done,
another five years of Cameron.
Milliband sacked for getting beat
Lib Dems eight, UKIP one seat.
Freed by Nick Clegg's night of woe
expect big changes to his manifesto!

In tow with the Yanks' hypocrisy
imposing unwanted democracy
Help finish the work of George Bush and his Pa, and mess up the rest North Africa

But worse than this could come alas
rocketing prices, electric and gas
hospital charges, binge drinking masses
rich pensioners riot on losing bus passes.
Malnourished children, beg for loose change
footsie one hundred all loss with no gains

Mountain top maiden strips brazenly rude.
God's been forsaken, to worship fast food.
Incense of grass swirling round sacred chippies
chills large assemblies, of fat bellied Hippies.

Separatist Scots spill over the border
northern counties in total disorder.

high on fried Mars bars, swilled Iron Bru
in unison roar "Independance D'noo"

"kill all the Sassanachs" while giggling out loud
makes you think on the whole,
they're not a bad crowd

But if made aware what causes the laughter?
opponents would not be so glad
For the wearing of kilts without knickers,
advancing through feathery grass,
has this side effect of tickling,
the most merciless warrior's ass.*

Meanwhile.
Just down the road to a break away group
sucking fishermans friends to avoid getting croup
Ronald Mac Donald, through booming loud speakers
grooms young men and girls, into suicide eaters.
Repleting converts from hot sweaty kitchens
Desciples behead... scores of infidel chickens.

Refugee numbers... thousands at most
abandoning homes, flee south to the coast.
Weeping children, terrified folks,
sail perilous oceans, in leaking boats.
Risking lives traveling far
for job and security in Zanzibar.
And if they survive, float anywhere near
get a hostile reception,
as their counterparts here.

This alternative prospect, is outrageously mad
and there's no chance we'll have
a future before us being so bad.
logically thinking, it's not hard to guess
how we got into, "another fine mess."

Present day life has been flimsily built
with ten parts of greed, to one of part guilt,
on foundations of patched up anomaly,
too many for me to rhyme.
wobbling on botched legislation,
thought "Good Ideas" at the time.

Our much loved seafaring nation
admitted, has much to atone.
But a couple of positive moments
deducted from times we complain
spent watching events on the telly.
would re-affirm again.

No matter who you vote for
before you moan and groan
compared with other regimes
There's *nooooo* place like home.

*A contributary factor in the rout of William Wallace

LEISURE TIME LOST

During my early life when it was a five and a half day working week, the only chance of a lie-in was Sunday morning. But Ernie Jones, a jolly drinking aquaintance and also Verger at All Saints Church, Rhodes, ruined my peace, tolling the bell for what seemed an eternity. The ringing of church bells is a far better pursuasive way to become a non believer than any of Richard Dawkins' logical argument.

Dawn, the Verger he arises,
combs his hair puts down soap
goes off in search of that dangling rope,
on which his hands will gladly blister,
for the benefit of those
without clock or transistor.

grim faced with each pull
then monotonous dong,
hoping to swell the pious throng
to which the Priest with fire and thunder
berates a congregation,
the choir outnumber.

Communion,
during which Jesus Christ symbolically munched,
is the ultimate devotion,
before retiring to lunch.

To the devil I would sell my soul alas
might it still that clanging
lump of brass

so on my lips
these words I poise
for Christ's sake
stop that... F***ing noise.

Epilogue.
Finally stripped of my Christian veneer
lying here in an angry mist
I contemplate life as an atheist
a reluctant Godless infidel
condemned forever
roasting in Hell
together with, I hope
that Verger,
and his bloody rope.

THE EDGE OF DESPAIR

This is my idea of what the onset of dementia is about. It could be you might think uninformed rubbish, and I've thought myself: How can a victim of this distressing condition be depressed if they cannot remember what they're being miserable about?

I've found a pen, and paper too
but I've forgotten who I'm writing to
Ah! It's coming back, the subject though
an appointment, at the Mental Health Bureau.
Not been out the house of late
with crippling arthritis, got enough on me plate.
Think I've got the date, and day alright
not sure it's, morning, noon, or night?

Feel peckish,
but the wife's not here to bake
not here to brew a pot of tea,
not here with home made cake
not here to say I'm handsome,
how many years it's been,
since our wedding at Saint Whatsitsname
faded photos on the green.
Life's ups and downs, the kids we had,
sticking together through good and bad,
have they been, my girl and lad,
what am I doing, with this pen and pad?

Wake in the morning skies are grey,
another bit aching since yesterday
my eyes well with tears, in the half empty bed
when it comes to me suddenly, she's long since dead.
Hell I'm hurting... lie quite still,
did I take, that cholesterol pill?

Got a wonderful Carer, she's the best,
gets me up in the morning, puts me to rest
prepares a nice breakfast, scrambled eggs,
but the toast isn't crispy, not like my Megs.
More angel than Carer, tops at her game,
is she previewing, her own future pain?
"A Saint in a pinny"
can't remember her name

This pen and paper, what's it for?
A reminder to remind me,
of things I'd forgotten before
did I mean to write a letter? – damn can't think
and compounding my confusion,
there's a meat pie in the sink.

Undignified, frustrating, the predicament I'm in,
SO weary of this wretched life *SO* want to pack it in.
Started saving aspirin planned an end to my despair
did I put them in the cupboard
can't remember where.

The children see me often always to and fro,
but they just don't seem to notice I'm desperately low
can't bring myself to ask them,
help me end it let me go.
Help me escape, this malicious thing
the constant roaring, tinnitus ring.
Help me desert my broken brain,
leaking memories it can't retain.

I WONDER

Would dinosaurs still be around if there had been good sewage disposal during the triassic period?

Recycle this, recycle that. renewable this renewable that
wind power, atomic power, all that and then
there's stem cell research for renewable men
all over the World, rubbish sorted, and binned
keen eco warriors optimism undimmed
blame global warming on cows breaking wind
whatever the theories, whatever the aims
recycling they tell us, will shrink carbon stains

I have a feeling of de ja vous
this has happened once before
when mighty dinosaurs roamed the earth
gobbling plants for all their worth.
And with lizard numbers soaring, as time passed quickly by
the once abundant forests, were in desperate short supply
soon where the green had been was a desolate scene
of barren dusty plains
and today can be found, lying on the ground
Dinosaur mortal remains

When all the food was gobbled up, enfeebled and horribly thin
failing physiques, bones beginning to peek
through gangrenous maggoty skin
with no food to stimulate weakening hearts
malnutrition and failing parts,
they finally choked on globe warming farts.

Disproving the theory that they might
have been made extinct by a meteorite.
This latest theory is probably right
an over-production of dinosaur shite.

But enough of this, get back to these times
with humanity facing an early demise
recycling this, recycling that, renewing this, renewing that
wind power atomic power, stringent new ways
could, postpone the inevitable for a couple of days
then like creatures of old we are poisoned, en masse
with a mixture of methane and sulphurious gas

Having cleansed herself of Dinosaurs, now begining on men
Mother Earth starts the process over again
slow, meticulous, without any fuss,
the cunning old bitch
recycles us.

WHAT A LET DOWN

This is a sad story of what could happen to anyone isolated in a community as a result of religious migration. Just as a matter of extra interest, I sincerely believe that when this is eventually published in the local Mosque Parish Magazine, complete integration will have been achieved.

Family gone life fully unfurled,
isolated, from the rest of the World
prospects exhausted changed population
Diocese closed
due to Christian migration.

Lone lady pensioner,
of limited means,
possessions few and meagred
out of place,
one left of her race
isolated beleaguered
bobbing grey head in seas of hijabs
enveloped with smells of rich spice and kebabs,
struggles with shopping, as best she can,
in a cold transfered corner from old Pakistan

Raising her eyes from the wet stone paved floor
sees a large notice pinned on the Mosque door.
"Because of the conflicts involving our lads
in the ever increasing sphere of jihads,

we're informed by the prophet
from Heaven up high
stocks of virgins have almost run dry;
so until such times this can be amended
suicide bombings will be suspended."

I've not much time left,
am here on my own,
she carefully thinks theorizing,
I'll see the Imam,
read the Koran
and prepare for radicalising.

I'm not much to look at
but when dressed and out
for a suicide bomber I'm better than nowt.
at least with a glance he can quickly gauge
I've been round the block,
and not under age.
He can do as he likes behave like a beast
and be safe from them stupid West Yorkshire police.

The local Imam thinks "what a prize"
her agreeing to be radicalised.
In detail explains as she winds on hijab
her noble first martyr
might've blown up his cab.
And to perform a good seeing to
is an honour
on a freshly exploded, suicide bomber.

In a state of excitement, uncraven of death
can't wait to expend her last final breath
begins to do things bad for her health
jogging swimming sapping her strength
in violent attempt to shorten life's length.

"CONVERT'S PREMATURE DEATH"
headlines reason
completes racial harmony, all round cohesion!

Whispy silks, draping fulsome hips
anxiously wait her hero's hot lips
At last here's the moment,
she's waited *SO* long
to engage this fanatic's
blood engorged dong,
they bring him contained
in a large plastic bin,
and say:
"sort out the bits you're most interested in".

THE JOYS OF APICULTURE

These days indepth research is essential before considering taking up Apiculture, with its thousands of employees.

Two bees flew into TESCO. while out at work one day
both tired agreed to rest a while before they flew away
recovering on a checkout, glimpsed the price of passing honey
Jesus Christ they chorused that's a lot of money
three pounds odd for half a pound that's a huge amount
we'll have to bring that bastard of a keeper to account.

We work all day for nothing, in flight over heath and stream
to return with royal jelly, for that egg laying, lazy fat Queen
no wonder we don't live long, a few weeks life then grief,
bet him and his wife share the profits,
the dastardly slave driving thief.
We must organise a union, and reveal to the World our plight
of exhausting long hours in the daylight
little rest in the brief summer night.

Emancipate our members then engage in dual pronged missions
demanding decent scales of pay, improvements in working conditions
equal rates for workers doing nineteen hours a day
sweating in hot sunshine, chilly when skies are grey

Plus a penny a time for her majestys eggs paid into pension schemes
and sodall for them idle Drones whose only task it seems
is arsing about doing nowt all day, between shagging future Queens

Another serious issue for Health and Safety to note
is the detrimental side effects from the use of passive smoke.
Unless they agree our conditions and we're paid by way of money
our response will be a work to rule slowing down the flow of honey.
We'll fly no further than sight of the Hive keeping well within its environs
restricting labour to ground hugging plants, daisies and dandelions.

After months of bitter dispute, infighting wrangling, rage
the strike weary hive and its workers were awarded the minimum wage.
In theory it was a great victory but, it didn't improve their lot.
Instead the price of honey went up to a million pounds a pot.
The result, an exclusive market, for them as 'as a big wedge
the only place that stocks it now, is a strongroom in Alderley Edge

It's good to know this commodity, is still within someone's reach,
although costing a little over, what the man of the house
earns each week.

For everyone in Britain today, the average home, on modest pay,
Breakfast time's dull and gloomy, limited most, to jam on toast.
Except for the likes of Wayne Rooney.

FASHIONS CHANGE BUT PEOPLE DON'T

This next poem is based on fact, the only incorrect part is the bit about the Verger's bell ringing, because during WW2 church bells were to be rung only in the event of a German invasion.

I've had a long life and at eighty five
thankful still to be alive
I gaze in the flames recalling when
impatient for Santa aged just ten.
Dad carried up presents in stockinged feet
treading loose floorboards made ominous creak
toys placed carefully on to our bed
Mechano, lead soldiers, books to be read.

Long empty months until Christmas
had climaxed to joyous peaks.
Now the years pass by so quickly.
seems it's here, every six f*..king weeks.

Life has evolved from "not quite to boring"
most of my hours spent sleeping and snoring
nightmare-ish with statin hyped dreams.
I'm back in the Army stood to attention
listening to language I'd rather not mention.
Five a side football in the School team
Victoria Baths, so cold I could scream.

Wounded soldiers from Broughton House
sat in wheelchairs at the Church dance
by the looks on their faces, given half a chance

would sooner be fighting
somewhere back in France.

During a tango one turns to his mate
saying what a way to recuperate
I'd sooner be blancoing kit in the hut.
Mate snaps,
"shouldn't have shot yourself in the foot"

Me and my friends in the Church Lads Brigade
shiny buckles, badges and braid.
drums a beating bugles blowing
what a stirring sight we made.

Hungover Verger claps ancient brass bell
the sonorous, single, repetative knell
is a prelude to parables how to avoid
the slippery slope to Hell.

Though times were hard and uncertain
our attendance was loyal and perpetual
comparing our Vicar to modern times
and thinking back to his basest designs
at least he was "hetrosexual"

That apart, a kindly man,
with always a friendly greeting
in particular for soldiers wives,
at Mothers' Union meetings.

On hearing accounts of nervous distress
lonely nights, anxious days, tearful yearnings.
he devoted more time to be extra kind
on alternative Tuesday's at half past nine
keeping their home fires burning.

Working days over,
each morn I turn over.
alarm clock no longer rings
spend waking hours getting weary
passing time doing please myself things.

I'm off to bed, but for one last chore,
if I go unexpected one night
That's deleting the recent history
on my tablets most visited site.

BEING KIND TO YOUNG CHILDREN CAN HAVE LONG TERM CONSEQUENCES

This is a tale of how mistaken parents can be when they ply children with nice things in an effort to frustrate anything other than happiness creeping into their little lives.

Drugs! what ever we think of them legal or not,
those prescribed by Doctors
will cure what you've got
after careful perusal of notes, he will
dispense what he thinks, the lesser evil

Illegal drugs from a street corner plot
will on the other hand shorten your lot
hooded dealer sells various highs,
to help sniffling Junkies
chase dragons through skies

We all indulge to some extent
the popping of pills rubbing ointment
a crying childs life made happy and richer
on ever more gobsfull of dolly mixture
ALL the time now, he's angry and tired
more and more Smarties, and wine gums required
out of control Mums got no money
mugs kittle sister for Easter Bunny
Mother steals for his hourly fix
at her nearest TESCO's pick and mix

In Court she pleads he's only three
please don't take him away from me
I'm the guilty one can't you see
I supplied the addictive candy
I was blind to see the trouble brewing
my good intention has led to his ruin

Summing up the Magistrate states
it all comes down to the old debate
happiness is not possible
the long term to sustain
with misguided acts of kindness
to a brand new baby's brain
toffees in moderation
are alright in their place,
but not as a temper distracter
to shut its little face

Any old Grandma will tell you
that if you really care
one has to apply deep thinking
for a baby's best welfare.

Suppressing moods with sweeties
in a young ones formative years
can mask more sinister reasons
for symptomatic tears.

To all potential parents
if your kids wake crying at night
spend time giving hugs and kisses.
Not a quick fix, with Turkish Delight.

ARMISTICE DAY

While I've been doing my stint down here on earth there have been astounding advances in technology, men on the moon etc. but all these achievments would not have developed so quickly had they not been precipitated by the advent of war as best ways of killing people, then in between wars modified to more peaceful pursuits. Why is it that mankind can develop so quickly in this respect and at the same time be so backward compassionwise toward their fellow creatures?
The question is do we need war to progress competitively or should we take time off getting to know each other better?

Every November we gather to see
a four generation old documentry
where everyone featured from that time and World
is a black and white ghost in the pictures unfurled.
Grainy spectres returned yet again
re-fighting, re-dying, re-writhing in pain,
for lasting peace, that with hindsight's in vain.
Examples of wills and letters are shown
of elequent content since vanished unknown,
the copper plate writing testaments fill,
betray an extinct, lost language skill.

Sombre Presenter with camera crew,
as Parliament's Ben chimes eleven
remind silent mourners lest we forget
young lives prematurely in Heaven.
Sounds of the last post fade through trees
heads bowed over lamentations,
falling rain dilutes the tears of assorted generations

Shattered survivors from distant campaigns,
salute chiselled out concrete moss filled names.
Then wended home on wheelchairs canes
mobility cars, cold zimmer frames.

At night to scramble over tops in dreams,
"JUMP TO IT LADS!" Sergeant Major screams.
Leaping over stuttering guns
hand to hand fighting, bayoneting Huns,
sons' and husbands' seeping blood,
drown in craters deep with mud.
Maimed and slain, in vain bids to attain.

A Will 'O' Wist unachievable
negative unbelieveable.
Ambiguous "Greater Good".

Nervous first year pupil with grave naivety,
reads out loud her essay, on our bellicose history,
listing recent conflicts, in the air, on land, at sea,
global wars, one and two, Korea, Vietnam,
Kuwait, Iraq, Syria, the murderous fake Islam.

Glancing round at her listening friends
differing complexions,
why oh why can't adults, like us,
work hard toward good relations?

Please Miss I'm confused, not sure I understood.
Will "WE" as well, have to suffer for –
And What is a *Greater Good*?

THE WINE IS ALL GONE, AND NO DEPOSIT ON THE BOTTLE

Poem number ten I suppose is a resume of key events in one's life that with hindsight suggests how we're all slotted depending on ability, to preserve the comfortable status quo of our betters.

Old man gazing at the sky,
Watching the nebulous and cumulus float by,
patches of blue, erratic Swift.
Ageing body vigour spent,
on ideas with motive, most well meant.

All those years, so quickly gone,
friends passed away, one by one,
days come and go each the same,
shame about Fred ... erm what's his name?
We were both in the Army Service Corps,
a deterrent they said, to for ever stop war,
reluctant conscripts, augmenting volunteers,
helped alay our leaders fears,
bullying Corporals, life abject misery,
hours of drill, regimental history,
scathingly told your Corps "a dead loss"
for winning just one Victoria Cross.

Thinking back and of Hitlers cause,
and what if we'd lost that most dreadful of wars,
the Worlds worst ever, bloody, campaign,
can't help feeling today, would be just the same.

Fighting, killing, avarice, lust,
uncertain periods of boom and bust,
bent politicians feather their nests,
bundles from lobbyists,
clutched to their breasts,
sitting, dozing, passing bills,
on family values, shortage of skills,
Peerages, Knighthoods, ever in mind,
Conservative, Labour, they're all of a kind

Cameron, Clegg, agreeing both,
on more investment, rapid growth,
deep in recession, down on our knees,
can't compete with those crafty Chinese,
with their smoking chimneys, air impure,
downtrodden workers, rich entrepreneur,
crowded sweatshops, blacked out sun,
toiling from dawn, till the day is done.

Buttercup meadows! May blossom in flower!
might we ever get back to real horse power,
magnificant shires harnessed together
iron clad wheels, creaking leather,
cottage industry, clement weather,
subsistance farming, unfiltered sun,
swarming bees constant hum,
hand churned butter, making hay,
work confined to the light of day.

Damn mechanisation, and all it entailed,
There'd be no global warming,
had the Luddites prevailed.

THE IN OUT OKY COKY

This is a little something I put together in in a failed effort to encourage a yes vote in the EU referendum. In a devided world with less security, the next and last war will only last the time it takes for a quick cuppa while awaiting the obituary that is the bomb with ALL our names on it.

Get out, get out, fat Boris shouted
hear hear, hear hear, Nigel eagerly spouted,
they're the ones who shout the loudest,
and say of Britain we're the proudest.

The likes of him and mate Farage
dismiss folks genuine fears
after all Nige'll still afford
his taste in fancy beers.

Extoling last century values
worshipping shit covered statues.
Political has-beens on chipped stone plinths
share prominent space with Peter Pan
and guam covered prancing Nymphs.

On bended knee, they fervently plea
to someone they're unable to see
watch over, our beloved Queen's
extended family.

As Farage and retro haired Boris
wind up their lets get out rant
hoping these isles, stay pleasantly green
and be never described as verdant.
Spewing misleading bollocks
praising corrupt old monarchs.

Each week a brand new hospital!
Nigel lustily screamed
he doesn't say
we could save as much
scrapping Trident submarines.
and might as well while at it
archaic Kings and Queens.

He should look into his history book
and since world war one discover
the British have been warring
in some theatre or another
each and every twelve months
of the recent century past.
Must we leave
and chance lose hopes
for enduring peace at last.

Not one month in those hundred years
went without a fight
the flower of our English youth
cut down in shiny boots
to feed some obscure trading war's
economic roots

If we were forward thinking and to stay in
all said yes
we'd have twenty odd potential
future adversaries less.
Never more to see in an English field
a bloodstained axe by a dented sheild.

The modern EU invader
treads ancestors undefined grave
as did his ilk before him,
thousands wave upon wave
he's not lately a blood thirsty savage
looking to rape and ravage.

Instead he adapts his belligerent crouch.
to harvesting
peas and cabbage.

It stands to sense that as prosperity builds and spreads throughout the European Community, the small economic nomadic groups will eventually drift back whence they originated to enjoy the standards of living we in these islands have un-appreciated for so long.
Leaving us to harvest our own turnips?
Or us (God forbid) digging theirs.

THE BEAUTIFUL GAME ???

The chief exec. of the premier league
dropped a ball playing verbal uppy.
Saying that dames shouldn't have any claims
on the beautiful game of footy.

Adding. Members of the opposite sex,
physically different, tearful, and tender,
Couldn't professionally like a man!
kick a Beckham match winning bender

A series of texts, slighting the fair sex
made feminists angry and furious.
Like this national gem, run by men
is genuine, open unspurious.

Our continued intent is to present
a game essentially manly.
Compared to the masculine rough tough approach
women's soccer is mamby pamby.
with varying levels of substandard play
the likes of at Accrington Stanley.

I must admit, he's right a bit
its effect on speed and mobility.
immediate change would have to be made
and applied with impartial rigidity.
A foul, "hypothetical" springs to mind
of a female who's generously fulsome
sprinting halfway down the pitch
ball secure in the cleft of her bosom.

Attending ladies football
after hearing the widespread renown
I wasn't impressed with the dribbling,
and hissed at a dissident's frown.
But to compensate for the slowness of pace
was their boobs bouncing up and then down.

Game nearly over minutes to go
ample left winger big breasted Flo
pounces on a long ball, just inside the box
as referee and linesmen check official clocks.

Setting in motion, a practice ground set piece
wrong footing crouching keeper prior to release,
boots ball into the empty net
past post and goalie's mitt
only to be ruled offside,
three quarters of a tit.

Proving. Tongue In Cheek.

Female conformity by design
was never intentionally made.
Trying to do what blokes do best
no matter how well played.

HO. HO. HO.

Did you all have a nice Christmas? This is a descriptive poem of the usual boxing day family gathering, starting off nice enough, but then deteriorating as well lubricated tongues are loosened by excessive tippling.

The party season comes around
families gather carols sound
Uncles aunties cousin Bill
pilgrimage to Grandma's bearing gifts with goodwill.
Assembled in the parlour comfy warm and snug
dispensing warm affection a kiss with every hug
children gaze in awe at the magic twinkling tree
and wonder what the present is
Santa's brought for me.

Dinner over table cleared guests drowsily replete
Many hands help wash the pots
tired Granny rests her feet,
guests primed up and fidgety
start the marathon drinking bout.
Voices swell in volume,
whiskey chases stout.
Girded loins anticipate
the annual falling out.

Afternoon fades into a cold and frosty night,
waxed up moon at fullness sends out beams of silver light
sentimental music keeps time to clinking pots
sleeping sibbling rivalry, awakes to set the plot
Uncle Stanley, hail and hearty

fancies himself life 'n' soul of the party
embarassed Aunt Myrtle with a glance t'ward nephew Jeff
downs a pint of homebrew without drawing a single breath.

Aunt Maizie sat sitting upset and overwrought,
mildly disappointed at the prezzy she'd been bought
leans into the company with an explanatory word
of the lies about her eldest they might possibly have heard
the slanderous gossip blighting her lad
his petty thieving, him inherently bad.
Those who said it it's them that's bad
got nowt else to talk about, they're well bloody sad.
He's loving, affectionate basically good
poor little buggers, just misunderstood
Aunt Jessie concurs she has a point.
As their twelve year old subject
sits rolling a joint.

Posh aunt Florrie with smart uncle Pete
come all the way down, from their country retreat
nervously silent while everyone sings
to hits by Sinatra, an album of Bing's.
Listening to my way they sit there and cringe
then Julie belts out all her favourite things

Stan staggers past, on his way to the bog
throws up on a couple out having a snog;
the resultant cartwheel from his slip on the grass
eclipses the moon with his flying fat ass.
premature night causes chaos on Mars
muddled up Sat Navs lose folk in their cars
Peturbed at the din, Uncle Tim rushes in,

informing the distraught Myrtle.
He's lay on the ground with his trousers down
on his back, like an upsidedown turtle.

In the kitchen meanwhile spraying the bile
sit three Aunties, big Fred, and a cousin
opportunities thin to get a word in
go at it, ten to the dozen
they make cruel jibes at the wart on Jim's nose
bitch about Pete and his second hand Rolls.
John the tight sod didn't bring any beer
that teenage dress, Flo wore last year
you didn't see it interspersed Ann.
Gave a new meaning to mutton and lamb.

As for her and Big Head out in the sticks
they're a pair of affected play acting pricks
a bloody big house, five acres of land
paid for from money supplying wet sand
But in spite of the money them throwing it round
their own pew in Church, the forrested ground.
According to local consensus I've found
"they think"
He's full of shit, and she's nowt a pound.

Dust gathering stylus ploughs a groove
for them still mobile and able to move
but all too soon even they
give in to demands of this special day.
Summoned Cabbies call each name
returning fares to whence they came.
Closing the door at the end of the hall

Dad responds with a wave to the last goodnight call
Gran sobs it's over unsmiling and grim
looks at the scene then quickly at him
lights extinguished quick as good cheer
leave unpleasant aromas of smoke and stale beer.

Just like last year "I told you as much",
nowt like Dicken's "God bless us all" slutch
we've been at it since daylight non stop until dawn
I could screw Tiny Tim with Gabriel's horn.
as for that lot of ours the drunken strumpets!
I'd give 'em the same
with his angels host trumpets.

While all on earth are sleeping sound
forgotten disc spins round and round
to sum up the party one has to say
in a Noble Art particular way
it almost ended a Boxing day

Alternative (happy ending) verse.

Closing the door at the end of the hall
Dad responds with a smile to the last goodnight call
Gran sighs "it's over"
God bless us all.

SPRING HAIKU

Sleep interrupted
by gardener's probing fork
cringing hedgehog stirs.

ACCIDENTALY DISCOVERING ONE'S TRUE VOCATION

Looking around the conference hall in historic Harrogate
we look a little out of place to other delegates
executives in pinstriped suits. eager to sell their wares
bear down on gullible visitors
with intimidating stares

The private housing Landlord
really thinks he's it
bet he can't rent out all his stock
without substantial profit

Which is one of the facts about Rochdale
we're enormously proud to relate
despite a permanent, impecunious, state
"absolutely skint"
tenants think as landlords
they're absolutely mint

Eclipsing our competitors
left 'em in the dark
made up for the half hour lost
In that cavernous car park
when the reason for my being here
to me, came crystal clear
it wasn't because of my oratory skills
but to carry all the gear

Puzzled people homeward bound to Halifax and Leeds
carry information packs
and packets of corn flower seeds?
not really essential for present day needs
would've enjoyed a lot more success ?
with a picture of MD Gareth and his R.B.H. address.

It's too soon to measure impressions made
after delegates talking and browsing
but we hope in the future, to see
a hundred yard queue, seeking properties to view
around Rochdale borough Wide Housing ... Association?

I'M JUST WILD ABOUT HARRY (By Queen)

Money isn't everything as you'll find in in this last poem about an extended disfunctional family living lives of luxury in various parts of the capital. With huge personal incomes they are also the recipients of housing benefit gathered from various tax sources including the 20% value added tax, and squeezed without exemption from the already empty pockets of the homeless and poorest of our society. Ironically, the poor and homeless, together with the rest of the population, are the legal owners of these properties.

What on earth can we do about Harry,
Sighed liz to her faithful Consort
try something a little more drastic said Phil
now he's been photographically caught
it isn't just hearsay in the papers she said
that we could easily sort,
grimacing at Harry's arse
front page in the daily sport

One considers his behaviour
as grandson of mine
completely unacceptable
for the next but two in line
us royals can't afford
this dreadful loss of face
we'll have to find a more permanent way
to put him in his place

In the sixty years of being Queen
never thought I'd ever dream
of in-laws, grandkids and nieces,

brazenly showing the family up
flashing their bits and pieces.

Not content with fine clothes silken hose,
diamonds, fast cars, shiny rubies,
the Duchess of Cambridge
got in on the act
exposing her commoners boobies

The trouble and worry we've been through
since Charley wed that bitch
the projection of wholesome images
frustrated with hitch after hitch.

Wales's biggest mistake after wedlock
was allowing her out of doors
for instruction on livery stables
from office, to mucking out floors
the tutor a cavalry major
confused Di with mixed metaphors
on various ways to get mounted,
with and without the horse

Behind closed doors
in Harrods stores
folk, gossip, pointing the finger
masculate cake and speculate
which dad spawned Jims Titian topped ringer.
Not only is that bad enough
for this cheeky Las Vegas binge-er
it's rough enough, and exeedingly tough
struggling through life ... Being ginger

IT'S GOT TO BE BETTER THAN LAST YEAR?

This year holidays abroad have an added risk of being taken to hospital not only with sun stroke, but with lead poisoning as well, with some nut making it more inclusive for you with his kalashnikov. So I'm thinking of going the opposite way in future.

The time has come around again
to pack the bags and fly to Spain
from biting winds, incessant rain,
red runny nose, rhuematic pain

Disneyland, Egypt, Darem salar,
Cyprus, Tennerife, Tossa del Mar
a much needed break, we all agree
to cloudless skies, the warm blue sea,
a tan, and free top up,
of vitamin D

Mass invasion by rowdy Brits
Bulgaria Italy, St Moritz
humungus bums, sagging tums
on rubbish strewn beaches kids cry and scream
overfilled litter bins, melting ice cream
startled gulls take nervous flight
from sunstarved bodies reflecting the light
off acres of shimmering, cellulite

I'm back at home now quietly dwelling
on an upset tummy, and below the belt swelling
for not included with the all in deal

were unwanted extras, beside drinks and every meal
no use now to gripe and whinge
after fourteen days of reckless binge
'cos an itchy consequence of careless erotica
meant a lengthy course of, antibiotic-a

So bugger hot countries with gnats and bees
chips with everything, and STDs
I'll try the archipelago, of Outer Hebrides
there'll be no annoying drunks, no overpowering heat,
no stumbling round the dance floor
to the disco's deafening beat
I'll be noshing suet puddings
stuffed with Aberdeen angus meat

Devouring deep fried Mars bars, marching down the street
to the skirl of traditional bagpipes, Drum Major's stirring beat
folksongs in the local, dancing reels in stocking feet
and the most appealing feature,
of this stay at home retreat
is crabs caught in the Hebrides
are the sort, that you can eat.

AN IDIOT'S LOGIC

This is a sad tale highlighting the dilemma most parents are faced with when the kids revolt against their carefully planned healthy eating regime.

The latest food fad, is for us to eat
organic grown veg and local meat
Get it down whilst at its freshest
Having reached the peak of best-est

But stop awhile and pause to think
this healthy produce if you haven't forgotten
is nourished by a mixture
of all things rotten,
smelly and impure
horrible germs and squirming worms,
in heaps of steaming manure

But are the children aware of this
when into their shell like ears you hiss
eat five large portions of veg a day.
to keep life's threatening ailments away

But it's not that easy and doesn't end there
won't eat their greens
and Mum's in despair
distraught distracted with cries and squeals
takes them to Macdonald's, for *happy meals.*

Beaming, joyful, satisfied sighs,
stuffed full of nuggets, and fattening fries
the ginger haired clown's won her kids' affection
with burgers chips, teeth rotting confection.

Mother down hearted on the homeward ride
full of guilt and punctured pride
wiping tears she cannot hide
reasons, it's the lesser ill
than stay at home,
infanticide.

THERE'S NO SUCH THING AS OBLIVION WE'LL ALWAYS BE AROUND IN ONE FORM OR ANOTHER

Have you ever thought like most people do that after all these millions of years there must be only standing room left in Heaven, even though in the early days it was reckoned to be exclusive to the human race? But think again. This world of ours has accommodated the remains of every creature that ever lived quite comfortably since time began, by a process of gradual reduction. So when you're walking down the street gazing at the grass growing between the flags, that grass is living off the broken down residue of your predecessors, from whatever form and time.

The passing decades erode away
passion for work, interest in play.
Thirty years since, a loyal hard worker.
now I'm an indolent, benefit shirker.

Freed from the rigours
of routine work ways
I started a business
to fill empty days
with a brand new, untried, vocation.
It's the practice of "postponement"
or, advanced procrastination.

For hasty decisions made right away
without thought of what might follow
you must delay, put off today
and think about tomorrow

Did you know ... that there's just one thing
we can't procrastinate?
It's the day you get to pass through
Saint Michael's Heavenly gates.

Recumbent stretched on my sofa,
pondering how I'll fare
in the un-put-offable next stage
when I give up breathing air

My first time incarnation,
as everybody knows
was the shape of a bouncing baby
with cute little fingers and toes

Got stuck into life's tapestry
began to weave the weft
and eighty five years later
nearly finished what little bit's left

Aged ten I'd lost faith in grown ups,
made friends with a villain called ted
wouldn't come in when Mum shouted,
wagged it off school, stayed in bed,
Joined a gang of little terrors,
full of mischief with "up your arse" cred.
they told me there's no Father Christmas.
"It's your Dad, that puts toys on the bed"
Been years since that information
put my psyche in a mess

recently, had a last session
for the post traumatic stress.

Considered now to be normal
having sorted me mental bits
though I still consider most people
unreliable, devious, Gits.

To kick start new beginings
based on logic, proven sound,
I'll soon have to make the final choice
burn by fire, or decay underground.

Reduced to rich dark compost,
or potashed by the fire,
our scattered precious rebirth
mixed with water will inspire
the continuance of prospects
we each in turn admire.

A summary of this poem,
in Aesop fable form
points out the simple reason
for what and why we're born.

The final incarnation
on this earth
for me and you.
is manifest as compost
on the shelves at B&Q.

CRY OF THE OLD REACTIONARY

In Middleton town centre
senior citizens cry and complain
they've gone and dug the centre up, all over again
I hear they say the Council, are going to at last
make it what it used to be
like in the distant past
a junction of three main roads
where shops were varied and good
leading to Oldham, Rochdale, Monkey town,
proper name's Heywood.

A neat triangular garden, verdant, vibrant, alive
made to be like it would've been, in nineteen thirty five
brightly coloured flora, green painted wooden seat
where weary old aged pensioners
rest tired aching feet
admiring ivy clad toilets, dahlias, and broom
post paying a quarterly power bill
at the electric and gas showroom.
Well behaved young people, parading up then down
between temperance bar, the Ashetton Arms,
dry horse trough, and sleepy old town

Do we "really" want reminding of those hard unhappy times
polio diptheria, smoking chimneys, soot and grime
rivers choked with frothy scum,
infectious smelly slime.
A short hard working, dreary life
between wars in plagued ridden times.

Laid under the churchyard, having died young
victims of fever, consumptive lung
complaints not covered, by the Saturday Fund
newborn deaths, one in eleven
life expectancy, fifty seven.
outlook for old folk, uncertain and bleak,
facing a future, paid ten bob a week.

Lost in her youthful halcyon days
of rainfree summers, blossom filled Mays
explaining to grandkids the leisurely pace
walking the monkey run, past Market Place
the hint of a smile lights up gran's loving face

Today's generation will marry,
and to wide eyed children recall
what it was like in old fashioned times
when summers were best of all

Why do we resent all things modern,
and with constancy dreamily yearn
for old times gone forever, never to return.
It's peculiar to the aged ... reactiveness of mind,
they'd suffer repeats of World war two
to be once more in their prime.

IN OUR IMAGE

On getting up one morning
God walked to the pearly gate
and enquired of Michael his doorman
how's it going mate?
I'm absolutely knackered, and wish you'd investigate.

Never known it be this busy before
them coming up here to Heaven
swept off me feet trying to greet,
everyone twenty four seven.
The flow is overwhelming,
we need bigger cupboards and shelving.
But I have a suggestion could quicken commuting
a couple of lap tops to speed up computing.

We cannot update, answered God loud but gentle
we must stay as we are, and that's fundamental.
I could stop a few wars to help your cause
and while I'm at it, went on
I'll extend human life, to over a ton
ban dangerous pastimes done for fun
while postponing the annual drought
lingering deaths will increase to six weeks
and sudden ones quickly phased out.

There'll be a deep cut in their pensions I fear
but the good news is, they won't come up here
I know it will work, you can take it from me
leaving plenty of breaks, for a cup of tea.

But the downside effects of my wisdom and power
will result as matters of fact
in that everyone here in reception will go,
on zero hours contracts

Mike, red faced with anger faced up to God
I've rumbled you, you're a tight-arsed sod
the so called all loving, Supreme Divinity
you've enjoyed the good life for all of infinity
with that other bent pair in the holy trinity.

Of my many ideas thousands at most
sent to you at head office by first class post.
Epistled replies, signed "Almighty host"
state.
After much consideration we're unanimous at the close
that improvements applied for impractical.
Quote from Holy Ghost.

If you wish to dispute the figures, said God,
in irritated tone
come up to my office immediately
and get Holy Ghost on the phone.

List your complaints to his Personal Aide
who will automatically say.
"As you know the boss is invisible.
and no one can see him today".

THE PASSING OF MONA McCLAINE

This next poem is a commentary of when Mother-in-law Mona died some years ago aged ninety-eight. And now being the oldest surviving member of the clan I've only just realised the significance of how this poem, written at the time, relates to my own future destiny.

Conceived in the year before nineteen nought eight
times fraught with war, uncertainty, depression
children running barefoot, World in deep recession
jobs were few, unemployment rife
woeful prospects for a brand new life
born in the reign of Edward the Seventh
through troubled times with George the Fifth
the rise of Hitler, and Loch Ness myth.

Escaped reality at the Pics
Astaire, Valentino, Garbo, Tom Mix
along a change of subjugation
to George, the stuttering Sixth.

Not paying much attention as the Eulogist rambles on
Raking over times long gone
my mind drifts back to her final year
suffering the indignity, of full time care.
Watching residents come and go
The odd one rocking to and fro
patiently enduring long hours of monotony
after Doctor Times merciful lobotomy
left her memory an ephemeral glimmer.
repeating over, and over again
how she hated Sunday dinner

Daily procession down to the lounge
watching T.V. repeats, and "Go Compare" ads.
quiet in chairs on incontinence pads.
I look into her eyes set in that benign face
and softly ask the question, do you really like this place?
her answer is a smile, as a friend is ushered out
through the atmosphere of lavender
piss, and brussel sprout

As days turned to weeks long months into years
after much laughter, worry and tears
bearing the burden of ninety eight years
she exhaled her last breath when the good lord beckoned
freed from serfdom to Lizzie the Second.
then respectfully carried out
from that damp warm steamy ambience of
piss, and Brussel sprout.

To Blackly cemetery, on a sunny day so fine
the only destination she'd ever been on time
ceremony over, Humanist paid his fee
we spill on to the car park
to a thirties melody
O Mona you shall be free. Oh Lordy Lordy
O Mona you shall be free,

We're gathered here at the Old Boar's Head
drinking beer and breaking bread
celebrating the life of our recent dead
Mona, the Worldly wise, family head.

Mulling over good times
with friends and contemporaries.
rekindling sweet and poignant memories.
Of summer walks with Uncle Andrew
trips to Blackpool on the coach.
Might her last years have been happier?
feelings of guilt, and self reproach.

Calcified bones, kidney stones
fluttering heart, dodgy prostate,
takes forever to urinate.
Find it hard to accept that "I'm"
another victim of Father Time, well and truly ravaged
destined to rest ... dressed in my best
boxed up, on a flower filled carriage.

As Pastor relates to family and mates
round a hole, within cemetary gates.
Of my life and fruitful marriage.
I'll lie eraised in a second hand haze
of lavender, piss, and boiled cabbage.

LEARNING THE HARD WAY

Before becoming envious and covetous of the seemingly idylic lives of one's contemporaries, take a closer look at your own, before embarking on a long potentially frustraiting circular of comparison, at the end of which dawns the realisation. You've missed nowt.

Woke up this morning opened my eyes
to a lovely, momentus, unique sunrise,
today hallelujah is like no other,
after thirty years of unpaid care
I'm burying my Mother.
The funeral's booked for eleven oclock,
then it's on to high tea at the local CO-OP.

In the leading car behind flower be-decked hearse,
approaching the lofty grey Minster,
can't wait to get it over with and be a raving spinster
Brothers, sisters, pretty nieces,
peer in dark corners at statues in niches,
Uncles, Aunts, surly nephews,
fidget impatient in carved wooden pews.

Feeling guilty, not a bit sad,
worse than that, deep down I'm glad.
The door is open the World's my oyster,
escaped from that choking three bedroomed cloister.
I'll find a man, go open plan,
buy a gas fire, chuck out the coal.
From now on for me, it's pure rock and roll

All things bright and beautiful, pianassimo sets the scene
to celebrate her nine decades, the loving wife she'd been.
Coffin bearers lounging, outside of guam and soot stained wall,
faintly hear a collared dove's, far off dismal call.
Wreath, proclaiming "Mother" leaned against wet stone.
In the company of others, on this consecrate pit of bone.

As decaying white rice and confetti
feed roots of a knot weed invasion.
Heads awkwardly bowed we walk down the aisle,
on this saddest of sombre occasion.

Gargoyles high on corners, gaze down at this random array,
of gaudy ill matching colours, on this light subdued overcast day. Inside on a paste board like catafalque
scattered with sweet smelling phlox
waits Mum in her trendy, environment friendly,
woodchip, faux brass handled, box.

It's eighteen months on, since she's been gone
and I've tried lots of things new to do,
been to the dance, a coach trip to France
subscribed to the Gym, had a brief romance,
decorated the house aquired a tan,
went dating online to find a man.

It was so disappointing, no one asked me to dance,
spent most time alone, on the coach trip to France,
I thought when I met him "the perfect match"

but he insisted our romance be no strings attached,
the Gym was a let down didn't give me a glow
among all those posers and perfumed BO.
Don't like the colour they painted my house,
despaired of finding a loving spouse.

About to give up got rid of the tan,
I'd sooner be pallied without a man
then I saw online "respectable male"
searching for unattached single female
"For close relationship loving and tender,
to share with nice person of opposite gender."
We eventually meet at the caff down the street
the guy's a gentleman polite so discrete,
charming witty a bundle of laughs
and on saying goodbye we exchange photographs,
my snaps of me smiling in France last December
"is this what it's like to be loving and tender"?
but "his" ruined my day the worst possible way.
Was one, of his blood engorged member

Home alone now, back in the house
deep down reconciled I'll not be a spouse,
my string of affairs, cruelly blighted,
all ended in tears, unrequited.
I'm wise enough now to appreciate
that on my own, in spite of no mate.
I've always been happy. This side of the gate.

PENSIONERS DEMAND THE FORTY-FIVE MINUTE HOUR

Went for a check up the other day
It was strange what the doctor had to say
between lifting me vest, and sounding me chest
says, I've good advice for you,
about passing time in retirement,
with its mandatory nothing to do.

You gave up work some years ago
for a life of leisure, and vigorously to
pursue a life of pleasure
filling years, with nothing to do
but it would indicate in your present state
that's not exactly true.

The condition you're in, being just that bit thin
and I'm sure you must agree
you've been flouting the rules of retirement
to a dangerous degree.
By not doing sufficient nothing
for a man of ability.

Not doing your obligatry nothing
combined with elements of haste
means a huge backlog of nothing
has built up,
you need to waste.

Retirement's a serious business
I cannot over stress
the art of doing nothing
needs concentration and finesse
it can be a bind, twenty four hour grind.
Not bad though, for forgetful minds.

Deterioration in the elderly brain
is a complex problem hard to explain
from a laymans point of view,
unable to recall doing nothing at all
the poor souls, don't have a clue.
Obsessed, with not having given their best
do yesterdays nothing anew.

Re-doing nothing, that's, past, and gone
is doing nothing, already done
serious research on the subject I've found
suggests a coming up shortage
of nowt to go round.

For this crisis to be tackled
urgent action's overdue
to build up reserves of nothing
before there's –
nothing left, not to do.

So look after yourself in retirement
wrap up with the slightest cough
working twenty four seven hard at nothing
means never ... another day off.

OOPs

As time time goes by, every significant historical occasion gathers its share of conspiracy theory. Here is just one of the many surrounding this particular chap.
Religion is just another undemocratic party with a permanent autocratic leader going under the acronym G.O.D. (Great Old Dictator)

This poem is a whimsical account of what might have been.

Would Christianity to its followers, be convincing and real,
if Jesus Christ had got off with an eleventh hour appeal
A petition from the people to Pontious Pilate's ears?
Would it bugger up religion for the next two thousand years?

Imagine twelve Disciples trying hard to see
is it possible, to come up with a plausible plan B.
Did the Scribes, the Apostles, and one or two Sisters,
write the present day text, the holy scriptures,
the flexible facts, and Chinese whispers.
Did as Dan Brown suggest in his Davinci romance
Christ grow old with a loving Spouse,
in a holiday home, in the south of France. Where they say, can be seen to this very day
his descendants, sons and daughters.
While Dads makes the lemonade twelve per cent proof.
The kids run around on the waters.

I'M GOING TO BE HAPPY EVEN IF IT KILLS YOU

Human beings are basically selfish and inward looking. For everything they do has to have an element of pleasure or self satisfaction. and is usually at the expense of other human beings, and ever more exploitive of the other creatures we share the planet with. This poem illustrates how human selfishness persists late into life, with the gratuitous exploitation of anything animal or material, in a usually futile effort to distract from the mandatory discomfort that accompanies old age.

Feeling lonely on my own
methought I'll get a pet to own
but the usual sorts can't habitat
a Rochdale Borowide sheltered flat
we're banned from keeping dogs or cats
'cos they pooh on the staircase,
carpets, and mats

So a choice of small mammals that we could bring inter
good for old men and lonely sad spinster
was pinned to the wall, for us to consider.
half the trouble of kittens and curs
easy maintained, light on the purse
and most of all blessed with
tiny sphincters

Hamsters budgies white mice and rats
poor substitutions for pet dogs and cats
gerbils newts, parrots that talk,
peck who go near them with deafening squawk

Great for curmudgeons and nagging old cows
always on hand to join in with the rows.

Favourites included are birds in a cage
ideal and easy for those of great age
put in a corner, don't take up much roomage
hopping on perches flaunt colourful plumage
plus beautiful songs sung dependant of breed
on cups of plain water and the cheepest of seed.

Had a tortoise for a bit
used to think the world of it
but advanced in years and prospects grim
I found it hard to keep up with him
if he could have slepted
ALL year round?
our relationship would be perfect and sound
but conditions worsened to unsatisfactory
and off he went to the button factory.

When he'd gone I washed his dish
then suddenly thought, I'll get a fish!
there'll be no more mess to wipe off the floors,
no upping and downing opening doors
no need to bath or comb its hair
no brushing fish scales off the chair.
And when he snuffs it unlike a mog,
budgie, canary, rabbit or dog
it just takes a minute
to flush down the bog.

A SIMPLE EXPLANATION OF THE WORLD'S PROBLEMS

Global warming is the buzz topic of today. Its causes have been explained in many a disputed way. Here's my take on it:

I don't believe in God an atheist am I
another creature to come then die
as the infinite aeons pass slowly by.

I'm just one of many billions
who unconsciously conspire
to an insidious infection
a poisonous toxic culture
on a perfect breeding ground
spreading on life's matrix
devouring its helpless host
then blowing out pollution
like you do
after beans on toast.

THE LAST BUT ONE MOVE

It comes to us all in time the kids have flown the nest the cat's dead, rattling about in an all but empty house you think it's about time to downsize.

Having grown old and lost your Spouse
you think, good idea, I'll sell my house
and move to a new more comfy location
in Warden controlled accommodation.

Where you discover others who have lost their mates
and are well past recommended use by dates.
Ravaged by the passing of time
have grown feeble in body, and mind
and as they further degenerate
tend to others irritate
with tales of woe and yester-year
much to the annoyance of the targeted ear
that aches, as he or she garbles
to impatient ones, yet to lose their marbles.

So beware you people of sound mind
to whom the years have so far been kind
be patient, tolerant, toward those who harass.
Ponder the thought
that as time passes by,
YOU'll be a Pain in the upper thigh.

ELECTRIC DREAMS
THE UNAWAKENING

Would you believe me if I told you this was true? It centres on an electric bed like the one I've got. I'm afraid to use it now.

Looking up from the advert in the paper where she'd read
it was the latest thing in comfort
a modern electric bed
"The most up to date sleep machine
you could ever aspire to possess
Plus!
comfort only dreamt of in the arms of Morpheus

Discarding the empty tea cup, wiping her greasy lips
"thinks" could be the start to an era
of peaceful comfy kips
giving my Bert relief
from painful unsightly varicose veins,
and constantly aching hips,

Trembling with excitement as she clambered on the bus,
bought herself a ticket to the nearest Beds 'R' Us
assured by oily salesman
knicknamed honest Gus.
What she'd read in the local paper was accurate and true
and that honesty is our policy
at this quality bed venue.

Your fantastic aquisition, he added,
with a sly wink to his boss
will be at the door to meet you
as you get home off the bus.

At night while she watched Eastenders
Bert toddled off to the pub
where he joined a wedding party
and drank much more than he should.
Arriving home at twelve thirty
much the worse for wear
Gladys led him to the staircase
with a down trodden look of despair.
Staggering, arms round him
toward the bedroom door,
a task she'd done dutifuly, many times before
pulling back the bed clothes
hoisted him on to the bed
gently placed the pillow, under his balding head
whilst hoping she'd not wasted money
on this hi tech. millenium bed.

On returning to the kitchen
she buttered two slices of bread
sat down to watch big brother
followed by Sean of the dead.

Meanwhile in the bedroom, Bert lay fast asleep
in a bed so warm and comfy
didn't need to count any sheep.

Dead to the world,
bladder stretched beyond its limits
began to leak between the sheets
shorting all the electrical gimmicks.

Snapping tight shut this wonder bed
generating heat
encompassed the whole of Bert's body
except for his head and feet
then started to braise at mark number eight
ideal for a cut of tough meat.

Rushing up the staircase
full of foreboding and fear
cursing the man responsible
for inventing that Devil's brew beer
on entering the bedroom
Gladys realised with dismay
what she'd smelled was her old man cooking
not the local take away.

The coroner an amateur expert
on fine foods and TV cooks
summed up all the evidence
as if out of a recipe book
delivering his findings, eloquent, firm, and loud,
In a manner Nigela Lawson
and the Hairy Bikers would be proud.
"He" was braised to gourmet perfection
on a setting ideally low

With delicate flavours of sweaty feet
and underarm B.O.
One interesting, but needs to be mentioned fact,
was marination from the inside
by an infected urinary tract,
I hope lessons learned from his passing
do not go amiss,
my verdict based on clear evidence
conclusively is this.
The wretched man was poached to death
on a mattress soaked in piss
accelerated I'm sad to relate,
by electrically charged urine
from a leaky old prostate.

What rejuvinated Frankenstien
on Bert had the opposite effect
arcing from bed post to big toe
and earthing somewhere off his neck
the one redeeming feature
that might alay the widows grief
is to find out if,
the power on that awful night
was at the night time lower tariff.
Further assistance from public funds
could also be in the offing
for the extra financial burden incurred,
by a seldom used V shaped coffin.

Following a silent pause ...

the court erupted with spontaneous applause
in response to the Coroner's compassion.
The resultant publicity rippling wide and far
led him to be awarded
the M.B.E. and bar
and appointed restaurant critic
on the staff at the Morning Star.

June 2010

HOW TO LOSE FRIENDS (trying to) INFLUENCE POETRY

After you've read this I can hear you all cry: Why doesn't he take his own advice then?

Reading the work of some Poets I find
the enigmatic language used, hard to define,
why are their creations
in language rich and fine,
all but, indecipherable
and total strangers to the rhyme.

It's alright if you're clever enough
to have a surplus of words 'n stuff
through which to mentally trowel,
a rich vocabulary is of no use at all
if it comes out meaningless babble.
Write something witty, simple,
makes good sense,
not spontaneous rantings
in a state of crapulence.

So please budding Poet
thrill me, delight me, fill me with fears,
exhilarate me, scare me, reduce me to tears
lilting verse, soaring pros,
not a catalogue of wordly woes
domestic violence, tortured souls.
Think happy, while teasing out to find.
Those couplets, odes, and stanzas
recessed in your mind.

AN EXERCISE IN PUSHING ONE'S CREDIBILITY

When I first started to publish poetry on line I got absolutely no feedback whatsoever. So in desperation I wrote this next bit of rubbish in less than an hour and on being published it received two very favourable comments. To me though it doesn't make any sense at all. So I re-entitled it. What do you think?

Long straight rivulets of light,
flowing out into the bay of night,
returning on the back of dawn,
o'er skeletons of long ago forms,
a wretched heap of memories and fears,
moistened by a sea of loved ones tears,
happy times forgotten in the daytime bright,
return again in the after light,
to briefly stay before returning,
on those rivulets of memory rising,
alone, sad, miniscule, finite,
in the vast consuming blackened void
that is the bay of night.

GOOD TASTE

This poem puts me in mind of my Grandma in the thirties between the wars spitting on tissue paper the shop-keepers used for wrapping bread and then rubbing dirty marks off our hands and faces.
The basic hygiene of the time left a lot to be desired. But on the other hand, manners were impeccable.

My Granny's once good sense of taste
declined with an alarming haste,
can't tell the difference now between,
curried chicken and harricot bean
the reason why this happened
you'll often hear her say,
"I killed off all my taste buds
smoking sixty fags a day"

Her other thoughts of the gastric kind
are does it matter when ones almost blind
And cannot identify whether
you're eating a dish enjoyed in the past
with a gob that's morphed into leather

To quote my Granny once again
about the time she was eleven
she said, fish and chips don't taste the same
like in nineteen twenty seven

A time rich, she said, in polite respect
and friendly courteous ways
of endless nice weather,

children playing together
on happiness ridden warm days.

Wonderful fun under a sun
filling the empty blue sky
eating jam butties, drinking pop
Dad having a beer, Mum knitting sat near
So innocent and chaste.
And as we clear up to take our leave
Father, discretely, burps up his sleeve
A gesture performed
in old fashioned, good taste.

IT'S A GOOD JOB EVOLUTION IS A SLOW PROCESS

Some years ago, if you remember scientists found a way to clone sheep and cattle, and a big fuss was made when one of these unfortunate creatures found its way into the food chain. This poem illustrates how much earlier God adopting the cuckoo method used Mary's surrogate nest to produce his son without all the nastiness we mere mortals have to indulge in.

Oh what a fuss there're making now
about a dumb genetically cloned cow
identical to a natural bred creature,
exactly the same in every feature
nothing exceptional, ordinarilly plain,
slipped accidentally?
in the food chain

This humble animal with cloven feet
reduced to various cuts of meat
publicly villified, with extreme views,
born without sin
like the King of the Jews
jeered, abused, misunderstood,
but since epitomized to be all that's good

Unlike our lowly bovine whose destiny would,
play the main role in
a steak and kidney pud.
A two year old non-entity
remembered for dodgy paternity,

a pleasant repast served on a tray
a soon forgotten take away,
served with curry, rice, crisp popodum.
no everlasting martyrdom.

The time has come when we must now
empathise with this much maligned cow
her born from a test tube,
he a surrogate mother
both conceived
sans a bit of the other.

Assessing each ones worth
their short existence here on Earth
"the ox"
one's appetite to briefly stay
"the man"
devoured each holy day
by Catholic, Protestant, semi skilled Lay.
pursuing an impossible mission
to right past wrongs, and expidite
mans backlog, of contrition

The brightest bio-chemists
I hope can never win
and eliminate conception
side stepping original sin.
Life started in a kidney shaped tin
from harvested bits off your own kith and kin.

Without the slap and tickle
as in old style re-creation
sex would drop
to a poor third place
behind drugs and inebriation.

Take comfort from the thought that.
drinking is a pleasure,
in time, that knows no limits
compared to the old fashioned sex act
that with most men lasts all of... two minutes.

A MOST UNWELCOME WATERSHED

On being born a human being can be compared to a freshly inflated ballon, and just as an inflated ballon loses air overtime from the little appendages here and there on the surface, do men also, during the irreversible natural process of atrophy. If you're wondering what all that was about. It's a sincere but clumsy metaphor used in an effort to de-disgustify my next offering.

Goodbye my friend I'm in despair
to see you limp and lying there
great buddies since our early teens
enjoyed good times in crisp blue jeans

Loved, adored, of far and wide renown
shared erotic pleasures with the girls in town
each responding to fumbled endeavour
wished those star filled summer nights
were infinite, forever.

So sad to see my friend so still
neither bedside manner, medicine, or pill,
could bring back the strength, vitality, the will,
that might restore him vertical
vain efforts returning to past guile and stealth
heart breakingly unsuccessful,
on The National Health.

A tearful probing question
to an understanding Nurse
brings a semi professional answer,

(she has a knack of replying in verse)
this condition is known as old man's curse
"It's a sort of rigor mortis" she said, only in reverse
from a part of one's anatomy
that's provided years of bliss
can't negotiate the passage now
of some promiscuous Miss
downgraded to a waste pipe.
though still essential, for a piss.

Old, bent, wrinkled, and tired,
useful shelf life all but expired
no longer upright proud and admired
needs supporting from a stick
well what d'you expect
from an eighty year old prick.

DOING ONE'S BIT (although reluctantly)

I heard recently that the Queen is a fervent Boris Johnson disciple after all she has a lot to fear, for if we vote to stay it'll be a step toward a united republic of Europe. Worse than that, where's she going to put all the furniture when Jeremy Corbyn puts her in sheltered housing?

Queen Elizabeth arose one morn
into the eye of a political storm
a letter from the Chancellor, with a plea to her once more
set a prime example for Britain's rich and poor,
our Monarch, needs to appreciate and try to understand
that One's the top recipient of benefits in the land
and to understand the lifestyle One's enjoying at the present
is paid for from the pocket of One's average sullen peasant
One has to cut down on hairdos, the occasional dress,
In the wake of this latest,
percuniary mess
and be it pointedly pronounced with emphasized onus
that in the next years civil list
One won't get any bonus.

Damn she screeches in an foul mouthed verbal orgy,
snapping! "get my ...kin boots laced up"
before kicking the nearest corgie
I've worked my fingers to the bone
doing a forty hour week, on Ones own
without a single whinge, or moan
shivering up here on a freezing throne.

Dabbing eyes dry with crisp serviettes
stems tears that flow on her breakfast baggettes
sobbs, done this job for sixty years
and these are the thanks One gets.
After five long decades, as head of state
wearing this ponderous bling
my Chamberlain said,
I'd get ten per cent more
If I were a gentleman king.

Then going on tears in her eyes
says to dozing Philip
I'm blowed if all these vicious cuts,
will seriously hurt me or you,
I'll tell 'em I've suffered agonies
thinking this whole thing through
then pin a notice in the servants hall,
canceling their Christmas Do.
Charles can forgo a prezzy this year
'cause last year I noticed he
was happy and fully occupied
Talking to the tree.

I feel quite sorry for Camilla,
because of this enforced thrift
I'll have to to get back the deposit,
on that long overdue face lift
what to get Fergie and Andy goodness only knows
to get them the same as last year,
in hard times it's alright, I suppose,

for him, a tub of hair gel,
he enjoys being smart and slick
and a box of milk chocolate big toes
for her to suck and lick.
for Charles a stocking filler, he likes traditional beers
and large packet of sticky blue tack,
to pin back his rhubarb leaf ears.

Must get my honourable spokesman in chief
to repudiate the widespread belief
that Ones a scheming, benefits thief
by informing the local authority
in particular Housing chiefs
to stop Ones social payments,
and stuff the rent relief.
With all this off Ones conscience
we can sit down then relax
and think up a cunning alternative way,
of fiddling the council tax.

I'm sick of the bile, and malice
heaped on us here, at the Palace
That cheeky Chancellor, will have to accept
I will not be a Government tool
by proclaiming from midnight on Monday next week,
One will start a work,
NOT, to rule.

A SEASONAL STORY

Up sprang a gust of playful wind
scattering cherry blossom
in this May time spring,
swirling round legs
old and rickety
a scene,
of enchanting serendipity.

'Twas a canine's random scattered stools
transformed into petal encrusted jewels
euphemised on this fine day
when God's wonders combined to favour,
the droppings from a canine's
unsocial behaviour.

An accidental work of art,
forged by the elements taking part,
this vision of wonder, the soul to delight.
Blossom covered lumps of shite.

THE SEVEN YEAR METAMORPHOSIS

Young couples used to have long courtships of two or even three years, getting to know each other well before embarking together in marriage. Unfortunately today's generation do things the opposite way and after having met briefly marry quickly without getting to know each other thoroughly. This poem brings a timely warning to the unwary of the upset and misery a too hasty union could bring.

When things go wrong and sometime they do,
when he's being spiteful and making you blue,
When in a moment tense,
sarcastically infers to your lack of sense
wilting under insults and negative aggression
you sink into a long dark deep depression
cursing the love trap having long ago fell
compare it to a living Hell
when the realisation that this latest dispute
is nasty intolerance by that feelingless brute
reclining on a flattened couch
with bloated curry and lager filled pouch
upsets the peace with rumbling belly
while watching football on sixty inch telly,
nature films from overseas
marvelling at the size of Antipodean fleas
amazed at the standard of life in Australia,
scratches his arse, adjusts genitalia.

Thinking and musing of days gone by
that handsome young man
you, with so longed to lie

overflowing with good intent
an "Adonis" on marrying fervently bent.

Now guts bubble and swell in fetid ferment
from which the soon calm air to rent
a fart so loud and indiscreet
expelled by a shudder from head to feet
releasing gases rank and putrid
from vibrating orifice, loud, un-muted
face distorts with a pang of indigestion
as Chancellor Osborne answers a question
regarding the state of our ailing nation.

Fat faced, multi-chinned, unhealthy pallor
scruffy appearance, ignorant manner
uncomfortable, ill at ease,
wished he'd not eaten so much Chinese
that looked delightful on the plate
tasty with Monosodium glutamate

She washes the dishes then he clumsily kisses,
the cheek of his love lorn, neglected, "Mrs"
this greasy lip smack enriched with halitosis
is for her the completion, of his metamorphosis.

A TERMINAL TALE

This is a sad inevitable situation that everyone experiences during the course of their lives, an occasion logically acceptable after longevity. But tragedy when concerning a young life incomplete.

The Doctor being unable to mend,
utters with clinical, impartial dictation,
suspend all treatment and medication,
turns on his heel, vacates the room,
leaving Sister alone to supervise
her patients comfort and certain demise.

Tearful family solemn faced
praying in vain a miracle take place.
Watch loved ones suffering
anesthetized by death.
borne on a final, shallow breath.

USEFUL TO THE END

Most people of advanced years try to buy extra time by filling themselves with vitamins this is a perfect example of closing the stable doors etc. after not doing the things you should have done during the time you thought you were immortal. Seriously though, some do enjoy varying degrees of physical and mental betterment be it real or imagined taking these things. But the few who really feel better in every way are the people who sell them.
When the patient said his name was placebo, the psychiatrist demanded: "Well are you, or aren't you?"

To keep your sanity and be dementia free
imbibe copious doses of omega three,
supplement a diet that's alcohol free
with essential vitamins A. C. D. and E
this will keep you, serene and placid
eating porridge every day
boiled in fish oil fatty acid.

It must be right and good for you
was Granddads logical prognosis
one never hears of trout and cod,
dying with deep veined thrombosis.

It might thought he, guarantee great age,
go on to be be a wise old sage,
preserving a quickfire wit,
sticking to a regimes rules,
get healthy, fit, and slim,
miles of jogging every day,
plus a workout at the Gym

But Granddad's unproven conclusions
were fanciful illusion,
and on losing his short memory,
turned father of all fools,
with a side effect from his vitamin diet
being multi coloured stools.

Inevitably, but reluctantly Grandpa gave up the ghost,
and summoned to appear, before his almighty host
quaked as God boomed out with bored impartiality,
Horace! it's me that does immortality,
ME, the wise old sage,
the only thing WE happen to share
is you looking like me as it says in Bibles,
not far from that bit about worshipping idols
on... I just forget which page,

And a similar anomaly, as far as I can tell,
I by pure coincidence,
pass coloured turds as well,
which suggests a higher status for you a little bit
it's not a physical likeness mind,
more affinity in shit,

Which goes to show, he carried on,
"even I" as Heaven's King,
can't possibly be expected,
to think of every f..kin thing.
Oh! and a brand new commandment, we had to bring in
"Never mention, Richard Dawkin,

and that other prick, who's just as bad,
professor "smart arse" Hawkin".

Friends and family as you'd expect
solemn faced pay last respects
under cloud filtered sun and stars
gaze at the heart shaped tombstone,
(looks more like an arse)
on which lovingly graced in upper case,
chiselled with chest swelling pride.
THE ONLY ONE IN EXTRA CARE
WHO COULD WIPE HIS OWN BACKSIDE.

That's not quite right said an irate Nurse invited to the wake
in the last few weeks as his senses dimmed
I finished him off with a secondary wipe
'cause he'd only semi-skimmed.

Now there's a lesson to learn from keeping fit
no matter what your views,
wiping his bum, up until the end,
proved it wasn't all bad news.

As Gabriel led Horace to his new celestial position,
Grandpa looking round asked, with nervous inquisition,
I can understand Jesus and the Disciples being smaller,
but from what I've been told about God all my life,
I expected him... To be taller.

BAH HUMBUG

The only thing I now enjoy
of the Christmas celebrations
is the wearisome delight
on reaching twelfth night
taking down the decorations

Packing baubles folding garlands
vaccing a crumbly settee
plucking the dusty fairy
from astride her prickly tree

What blessed relief at last
the poor dear must be feeling
as she's put in a box
for the next twelve months
while her inner thighs are healing

Happy and glad it's all over now
smugly thinks to herself on her final bow
where else could you work
just twelve days a year.
Aren't I the lucky cow

Tears trickle as I reminisce
of times, and friends gone by
what would I give, to see Christmas once more
through a childs
uncynical eye.

TEXT FOR TODAY

I've been around for 86 years now and along the way have grown from disliking religion to a positive hatred of it, and I'm curious as to how a large proportion of highly intelligent people can't see after a lifetime of intense religious compliance, the unlikeliness that there is a super-being responsible for everybody and everything about us. And why do folk have to belong in large groups for God to take notice of them?

Because You can be faithful to your God without belonging to sectarian or mainstream groups. Christian, Buddhist. Hindu, Islam, etc.
Disassociate yourself from Them all. "Be your own Church," the Church of, whatever your name is.
You don't need to be mob handed for God to listen, go it alone! that's if you're still an un-enlightened believer.
Potential, Sixty million idependant Churches in the UK alone.

Do not
Go to your grave, conscience heavy with the atrocity ridden pasts of these mind controlling deities, or would *gangs* be a more appropriate title?

The whole of today's civilisation is based on the rantings of voice hearing, glandular imbalanced, phsycopaths, each injecting their own bile ridden versions of disharmony into successive generations of the as yet uncultured new born innocents.

Dignitaries adorned with ridiculous clothes, silly symbolism, plaster imagery, ostentatious buildings containing only the air they encompass. Scrapyards filled with decayed relics of past devious kings, Popes, bishops, generals, statesmen. Personal histories (in most cases) incompatible with the qualities essential to be a so called God fearer.

Structures designed to fill with awe the feeble minded,
mixed emotions in the agnostic,
couldn't they have built something more useful. a hospital for instance, cries the ever questioning realist
It's much better going through life as a progressive scholar than as a simpleton "conditioned" stationary puppet
bent on destroying every alternative, other than one's own religious following
exudes the enlightened. Cleansed of superstition Prophet,

How can Governments describe their brand of democracy "as true"
when many leaders of these democracies
are influenced by the dictates
from the ethereal acronym G.O.D. (Great Old Dictator)
The longest ruling imagined autocrat "ever" in all his
non existent guises?

Governments cooperate by turning a blind eye to the Church's insidious method of indoctrination, from birth by self appointed, un-elected, fancy dressed zealots. Indoctrination carried out in establishments built on foundations of slaughtered millions.

Where else has so much brutality and mass murder throughout history been perpertrated, other than in the name of religious rivalry of one form or another?
Even today in our so called 'civilized' world this manipulated evil (derived from original good intent they tell us) in all its manifestations, is tolerated and persists, among us still.
Blinkered bigots in funny hats preach the implementation of, an unproven, (and never will be) grossly illogical, "idiots' alternative" to the more logical Big Bang theory, and Darwin's proven species research, most importantly.
Common sense tells us that life is perpetuated by the deaths of every living organism from rooted flora, to cockroaches and kings.
In an infinite recycling process.

The Earth's girth gets bigger in an irreversable expanding cloak of poisonous detritus woven overtime by Man's over exploitive husbandry in efforts to sate an ever expanding population's greed, from which all life will inevitably end one day.

God or no God?

A RHYME CELEBRATING HISTORICAL AND LATTER DAY POVERTY

Have you ever noticed on BBC four
When they're showing old movies from times of yore.
Black and white film of bustling folk
girls wearing clogs a pipe smoking bloke
women in shawls, boys with their mates
pouring out the factory gates.

And there on the street to welcome them
what today, would look dead queer
a man with a keg on a barrow
selling pints of beer.
Days labour over done and extinct
tired sweaty worker selfishly thinks
I've toiled bloody hard, and long today
any excuse to spend his pay
greedily sates his thirst from the keg
at home, hungry kids, gnaw the table leg.

Many years on, old men reminisce
of golden times, spent on the piss,
a good day out for half a crown
all day in the pub, and the the Bookies in town
meanwhile,
downtrodden wife depressed with lifes ills,
got no money, unpaid bills
despairs at her ever increasing brood
the bleak empty cupboard bereft of food
new born babe in third hand cot

cries for relief from his miserable lot
enveloped secure in urine soaked windings
struggles in vain, to escape, grubby bindings.

Things are considerably better now
no starving kids, lesss furrowed brows
a welfare state, re-distributed wealth
universal credit and National Health
computers, telly, the wonder of I.T.
make present day deprivation, comparitive luxury.

Even the poorest are getting fat
a neighbour I know's an example of that
each mealtime to him, is a serious mission
burgers and fries, pushed down his neck
add to his frightful condition
cream cakes and junk food crammed in his face,
first past the post in a calorie race
five or six chins, eighty inch waste
four hundred kilos, an obese disgrace
like China's great wall
can be seen from near space

Risks of using modern gadgets,
is now it would appear
exposure to the side effects, of radioactive gear
the mobile phone and its over-use, they say, is worst of all.
An aquaintance of mine fell victim to it,
while making a marathon call,
deadly invisible microwaves,

there's none so lethal as those
churned his brain into a liquid
that dripped out the end of his nose

It's not the end of this sorry tale,
lying half dead with an empty head
confined to a bed insulated with lead
the poor chap's paid for it dear,
they've worked out a way to feed him though.
but in no way it's brought him good cheer
it just prolongs his miserable life
via a tube, down his shrivelled up ear.

SUMMAT AND NOWT

I firmly believe that the World we live in today emerged from a combination of accidental events running parallel with favourable coincidence. And after years of painstaking research. I am of the certain opinion, that the present would be on balance, a far better place to live, had the Garden of Eden been sited between Rochdale and Halifax

Gazing round while out and about
I'm always thinking of summat and nowt,
Of life on earth, how it began,
the universal master plan
Was it wonderman beyond the Moon,
had nothing to do one afternoon
bored in a "nothing to do" depression
decided on a creating session
result, an empire Christened milky way
sun, earth, night and day
stars, sea, mountain, crater
ruled over by a single guy
God the "Great Dictator"

filled with people, same as himself
in body, and mind but with varying face
to swarm around his empty place.
A renewable race, he decided to make
spawned by Adam with Eve,
and a dirty old snake.
Via a naughty learning forage
eating stuff from the tree of knowledge

Adam removed his fig leaf,
an outsize one at that
then all three jumped into bed, and started to begat
kinky serpent eagerly watched,
this first time sexual grapple
Adam giving her plenty of top
she chomping away on his apple
panting, perspiring, moving the earth.
Serpent voyeuring wide eyed.
The World's first,
"soixante-neuf."

Forced to bring out ten commandments
when the mob got out of hand
causing lots of problems
in his new and promised land,
scratched on lumps of stone
pearls of wisdom every one
gave them to a jewish bloke,
and told him, pass 'em on

transcribed into a bible, the oldest novel ever
dire warnings in short parables, for instance not to ever
stray from the path that's straight and narrow
don't covet your neighbours, squeaky wheelbarrow
be good and kind, not a rotter
"it's sold more copies than Harry Potter"

Nepotism rules in this deity
all hard work and not much gaeity

sending down his only son
sprung from the loins of a well surprised mum
to preach the almighties New Style, dictum.
Guiding, persuading,
a crook to gently prod
devoted caring shepherd,
sort of one man and his God.

He's been ruling for ever, through terror and fear
longer than any Dictators down here
as past events and recent times show
ask Muberak, Gaddafi,
they ought to know

Sadly since time immemorial
man's been adversarial
reluctant to love and to mix.
And what if Eve had been lesbian
she couldn't have had any kids.
Only time for gay sex unabated
in the Garden of Hebden Bridge.

GARDENERS WHIRL

Spring time's here with May the most beautiful month of the year to start this condensed little item of the season everyone looks forward to. Summer.

Mole in hole, Squirrel up pole,
may is out, cast a clout,
deviding cloves, punctured hose,
rambling rose, sensitive nose,
sowing seeds, pulling weeds,
telly on, watch Monty Don,
continuous rain, what a pain,
plant biennials, split perennials,
touch of frost, dahlias lost,
come October, summer over,
unused tools, back in sheds,
snails take over flower beds.
less light to see now in the day,
bye Monty, Joe, sweet Carol Klien,
see you all next May.

THE LOT OF A TECH GUY

Today's modern technology is bad for those suffering delicate mental strength. So if your brain is the sort that easily boils over, you'd be better employed in a less demanding job, like sharpening pencils in Argos.

The lot of a Tech-Guy is not a happy one
ironing out frustrations of near suicidal patrons
bottling up emotions for customer relations
straining to do twelve hours a day
improving punters knowledge in some small way.

Listening to people's faltering accounts
of viruses pop ups too many bytes,
explaining cure and reason for computer hazards
'thinks'
can't take anymore
from these stupid bastards,
pasting cutting unfriendly websites
add to innumerable sleepless nights.

Girlfriends come then depart in despair
unable to stimulate his floppy software
break down in tears can't get him debagged
suggest a hospital stay
for a thorough defragg.

Lying within intensive care
relieved of the come a day pressures to bear
cocooned in round the clock protection

wakes one morn with a penile erection, that he unable use
causes a power surge so massive it blows out every fuse.
Rendering the equipment, he depends on since arrival
useless for this poor wretch's,
chances of survival.

Doctors, Nurses, and technical friend
frantic with worry trying to mend.
Press knobs, throw switches, bind bare wires
in efforts to start it before he expires
Consultant and visitors moist of eye
hear Tech-guy's anguished, pathetic, last cry
through his stethoscope monitored cough.

Have you tried switching it, on and off ?

THE SPY WHO BAGGED ME

This is a tale, a tragic tale of a poor chap being at a wrong place at a wrong time So be warned stay away from parties organised by people whose speciality is the art of intrigue.

You've heard of the spy found dead in a holdall
caused quite a stir 'round the corridors of Whitehall
newspaper accounts were wild and unclear
some said he was straight some said he was queer
they said he used make up, wore diamond and gem
spent leisure time in gay bars, with boss the anonymous M.

Explanations were heard with the Coroner's authority
of international espionage, Britain's dwindling autonomy
integrity, loose morals, trans-genders and sodomy.

The verdict at the close of this muddled intrigue
made out he'd been whacked by a jealous colleague
In a bag, in a bathroom, wet with mould
Foiling his effort, to come in from the cold
a way to dispatch the jury were told
being obsolete and extremely old
these days they're secured with handcuffs and padlocks
with a laser beam slowly approaching. the bollocks.

But I don't believe this version's right
I know what happened that fateful night
mixing the drinks inevitably incurred
lots of martini, being shaken, not stirred.

Trouble with parties in the spying game
and this is a well known fact
there's not a lot you can talk about
because of the secrets act.

The truth of the matter, can now be said
it was not a double agent that made him dead
the findings won't be published, they're unbelievably, unique,
new evidence from a witness reluctant to speak
revealed, last guest to leave, on departing didn't peek
in the tightly zipped up holdall for at least another week
a press release from MI5, admitted, tongue in cheek
he was just another ordinary bloke, invited off the street
and not the man we thought he was, "an enigma breaking geek"
but Southern area champion
at professional hide and seek.

LIFE'S NEVER THE SAME WHEN YOU HAVE ONE OF THESE

All through the day up until dawn
impatient babies wait to be born
mothers bear pain, anxiety, and fears
replenishing life in this vale of tears
each one unique in its own special way
goes on to be labelled
with name and birthday.

Ninety per-cent perfect specimens of health
one or two lucky ones born into wealth
a few will be clever a minority dim
most of them average at least to begin
some will stay slim others grow fat
with traditional names Tom Dick and Pat.

Mums and Dads look down with delight,
at the wriggling legacies
of some Friday night
out come cameras numerous apps
startling small subjects
with hundreds of snaps.

Grand parents stand each side of the cot
her with white wine him a pint pot
"Utterly wonderful disarmingly cute"
gabbles Gran excited, Dad smilingly mute.

"In all my life have I ever seen
such a perfect new born beaut'"
Father nods in agreement
stood swaying pissed as a newt.

Grandpa not good at speaking,
complementary things
causes upset between parents
and the rest there assembled to cringe
slurring!
she certainly is a smashin' result
from a night out on the binge.

BUYING A SECOND HAND CAR CAN BE A DODGY UNDERTAKING

In the old days before civilisation when creatures died they were left where they dropped to break down and continue the next stage of their existence in a less sophisticated role.
Don't know why I said that, maybe it's because the next poem reminds us how far we've improved disposing of the dead.

Beware before you purchase
an ex-Mortician's hearse,
attracted by low mileage
and gentle lower speed
you'd be a mug
the glib advertisment to heed.

Don't be fooled by mint condition
and shiny mirrored body,
the absolute opposite
of marked and shoddy.

What the salesman omits to tell you
is over five and twenty years,
the inside's corroded and rusty,
from oceans of customer tears.

DOES LIFE REALLY BEGIN ON THE BOG?

Beholding this small corner, of our universe from space
you'd be tempted into thinking what a beautiful place.
Shining in the darkness, blue, indigo, bright green,
an awe inspiring sight, precious few have seen,
clothed in vegetation enclosed by rolling seas.
Spinning in the blackened void, with Jupiter and Mars,
criss-crossed by glowing comets, sparkling shooting stars.
Observed with wonder from afar, this big-bang one-off treasure,
whirls around, lit by the Sun, in unhurried timeless leisure.

But all is not well in this paradise apparent,
adding credence to the saying "Distance lends enchantment"
For in among that beauty on approaching ever near.
One day as craven quarry, then predator in turn,
hide millions of species in a World of perpetual fear.
On a shrinking dearth of precious earth,
frightened creatures thickly cover,
their only joy is original sin, apart eating one another

All of life God sends down, ends up cremated or in the ground.
As each generation completes its stay. spent, used, wrinkled, grey
It's squeezed out the arsehole of its host the Milky Way.
Processed into viscous handy size turds,
from all walks of life, Numpties and Nerds,
teachers, professors, Kings and Queens,
those out the jungle, and other Has-beens.
More useful dead, than when alive,

working for ever now, not nine till five.
Pulped together gristle and brain
feeding renewables over again.
Holy men euphemise "its glorification"
Thinking man reasons, "reincarnation"

Take for instance when an old man dies
it's hard to believe this waxen faced guy
once the darling of his Mothers eye.
Interred at the foot of the old apple tree.
morphed into bonemeal to eventually be,
plump ripe fruit for a recipe.
When the soul begins its journey, to Heaven way up high?
What's left doth swell the autumn fruit, for many a tasty pie.

Our remains are key to continue, rudimentary life as a whole,
Re-eaten, re-fined, then re-shit through,
subsequent lines of arse holes.
Posing yet another question, to prove this dissertate sound.
does God "really" work, among stars and things?
Or here down on earth making spring after spring.

WHAT CAME FIRST: TOURETTE'S OR BAD LANGUAGE?

A sympathetic GP can confirm your status as one of society's disadvantaged runts by opening the gates to Benefit Shangri-La with a stroke of his pen.

Simple minded person sits watching the TV
Sees her favourite characters
latest fashion malady
Identifies the symptoms
Shrieks
"that's what's up with me"
phones for an appointment
At the local surgery

Elderly Doctor can't be arsed to disagree
Confirms the diagnosis
between sips of tepid tea

Thinking, being a Doctor now
isn't what it used to be
curing tangible disorders
symptoms you can see
like adolescent acne
arthritic swollen knee
doing home visits,
comfort patients in their beds,
now the job is all about
"sorting muddled heads"

One obnoxious brat I know, and can hardly bear
looks on his Tourette's complaint
as a year round licence to swear
and on reaching puberty, he will without a doubt
evolve into a licra clad, foul mouthed, lager lout.

His mother's not much better
registering innocent pleas
blames persistent thieving
on deep seated O.C.D.s

Another crippling affliction
to a far more serious degree
is that society rotting virus
"benefit dependency"
for which there seems no cure,
a most discouraging prognosis.
Palliative care every seventh day
keeps dangerous urges to work at bay
with money prescribed in large doses.

ONE LAST INDULGENCE

The slowest period of time for me and I think most young people will agree is that interminable devlopement period between the ages of thirteen to eighteen, the adolescence years, when we all ran round shouting "I didn't ask to be born".

On reaching adolescence
my tastes were changed in Christmas presents
threw out all my Rupert books
toy cars, mechano set
expecting that from now on, I'm in future going to get
grown up gifts of, money, jewellery, and clothes
no more little action men, anything like those
no more jig saw puzzles, brightly coloured balloons,
now I'm looking old enough
to go in Wetherspoons.

Boxing day get out of bed don't feel very perky
retch at the smell of yesterday's beer, Chrissie pud and turkey
wilted broccoli, soggy stuffing, cold limp brussel sprout,
regretting my decision now, to ever have gone out
feeling slightly better, after an hour and a half's quiet grace
put on the coat, rush out t' Pub in trembling panicky haste.
With just an hour, to line em up
and get back off me face.

Now that I'm a creaking old man
going to treat myself, to a funeral plan
shall I choose a polished casket,
or environment friendly whicker basket
it really doesn't matter when the hooded Reaper knocks
might just as well be planted,
in an empty cardboard box

IMAGINED SCENARIO SOME TIME LATER

Solemn faced Mortician leads ancient horse drawn carriage
the only time I've gone away
without the need for baggage
clip clop, clip clop, slow measured pace
bystanders mutter, he was a waste of 'kin space
a circle of my closest friends, the majority agrees
that throughout my lazy workshy, indolent life of ease
there was a group of people, I'd enriched and really pleased.
The Directors, staff and workers,
at Brewer, John Willy Lees.

A solitary black clad mourner, eyes overflowed with tears
brings me to doubt our friendship
of five and twenty years,
the motive behind his welcoming smile,
and what it *REALLY* meant,
this distressed, emotional publican,
respected local gent,
with wet sales down,
since my demise,
a whopping, ten per cent.

One final wish I had granted
on the way to my daisy roofed home
invokes memories of railways,
steam, hot ash, fossil coal.
Was the choice to ride with my back to,
or facing, the horse's arsehole.

GOD BLESS YER SURRH

This is a tale of a not very successful internet scammer whose first effort at cybernetic crime, resulted in him metaphorically picking his own pocket.

The post came early this morning
One from the bank with a warning
Please attend without delay
There's an urgent message we wish to relay
About your account and its state of play

Walk down the street in reluctant hurry
Profusely sweating, sick with worry,
Took all my willpower, not to puke
Last night's drink and chicken curry

Open for business I run in
employees anxious pale and grim
one young clerk, a Teller novice
blurts, he's been summoned again to the boss's office

Servile ready, for degradation
Paused at his door,
full of apprehension
Racing pulse, wet through vest
heart beating loudly inside my of chest.
How much do I owe the local Nat West?

He's on the phone, selling stock and share
gesticulates to an empty chair
ends conversation, turns to me
countenance set to severity

There's iniquity afoot, said he,
in the depths of your account
huge deposits coming in, nothing going out,
it's not the usual pattern, and as far as I can see
someone's gone and stolen, your identity.

It was no one from Nigeria, or Jack the lad from Chad
we thought it might be you at first,
"but we don't now"
aren't you glad!

We've traced the rogue to Ireland, in the County of Antrim
this would be Irish felon was traditionally dim
it seems he bought your bank details, together with the pin
but instead of draining your account,
he's putting money in.

CHRISTMAS RECOLLECTIONS

This is an accurate account of events that happened on the nights of 22nd and 23rd December 1940 when as a ten year old in Manchester I experienced two twelve hour air raids on consecutive nights. The memories of which are still vivid in my mind. But I do not remember at all, any details of the Christmas that followed.
There were many other air raids on Manchester throughout the war, but these two were the most significant for me, resulting in the deaths of a school chum, his family, and neighbours. killed celebrating a childs fifth birthday.

The day after next, is Christmas Eve,
just been to Sunday School
we sang away in a manger,
and prayed
kneeling down on a stool,

The Vicar scolds us for giggling,
during prayer at this sacred event
it was summat 'bout incense and donkeys,
or shepherds in a tent,
then we were given Bibles,
mince pies, and watery tea,
Not *MY* idea of what,
a Christmas present, ought to be

Wanted a colouring book with crayons,
model spitfire,or a pen,
But the angel said nowt about children,
when he talked of goodwill, to all men

Far away in Europe,
the lowlands, Belgium, France,
Germans load up aeroplanes, with deadly ordenance,
little did we know that day,
singing Away in a manger, 'n where Jesus lay,
three hundred bombers were on their way,
orders to kill with malicious intent,
the absolute opposite,
what Gabriell meant.

Halfpast six, the sirens wail, we're sat down having tea,
I'm balancing a bowl of wartime cereal on my knee,
father says be quiet, keep calm,
it's more than likely a false alarm
we sit down then,
mum says it might be Liverpool again,
little did we know that day,
it was to Manchester,
they were on their way.

Sounds of the siren fade in the night,
Luftwaffe approaches, flight, after flight,
guns blaze a reception, flares brighten the sky,
innocent people, about to die,
bombs fall on cobbles, from ten thousand feet
folk in terraced houses,
perish on moonlit streets.
Whose children, some shy, some revelling in glory,
before doting parents, just hours before
had enacted, the Christmas story.

Dispassionate aircrew relentlessly pound,
Trafford park, Pendleton, Uniteds ground,
anxious rescuers, sight blurred with tears,
dig for survivors, realize worst fears
children in death, crowned with tinsel and blood,
water gushed from shattered pipes,
turns earth to clinging mud,
burning gas escaping mains, illuminates the scene,
broken bodies share a crater
once a loving home had been,
with apples, nuts, toy soldiers,
Grandma's, china, figurine.

They come again the following night, twenty four hours in all,
rekindling dying embers, as showers of incendiaries fall,
bomb doors gape open, unleashing a second load
compounding yesterdays misery, for young, and old
thousands are injured, six hundred die,
From death and destruction, there is no reprieve,
during terror filled hours,
into Christmas Eve.

Looking back those seventy five years,
can't think of another time when,
we chose the option not to wish,
Peace and Goodwill,
to all men.

NEVER THOUGHT I'D SEE THE DAY

This is about young mum rivalry concerning baby development.

Looking lost in Wilkies store
while out buying bread
an enthusiatic salesgirl
sidled up to me and said:
If you're looking for a bargain sir
these skeleton suits are cheap
got too many in for Halloween,
just took them off the shelf
I said,
I'm not wasting cash on that
I'll be one soon meself.

Overheard two mothers talk
of kids and what they say
things that would appall old folk
If they were here today.

One said baby Daisy's
coming on in leaps and bounds
she's aware of all the colours
can identify most sounds.
eating meals all by herself
and last week gained two pounds.
Remarkably intelligent, especially at grammar
and just approaching six months old
when she said her first word "Mama"

Riled by all her boasting
and not to be out done,
her mate began to lay it on about HER baby son
his identifying colours
his bigger leaps and bounds,
spending hours on the lap top
repeating different sounds
and, to top it all amazingly,
last week gained THREE pounds

I imagine him in cap and gown
a potential brilliant scholar,
aquiring in time, I'm sure, she said
a PHD in grammar,
to illustrate how bright he is
compared with other prodigy
forecast that he, would get a degree,
in the most difficult, to learn about ology.
He's more intelligent than me said she
heaping on the glory
going on to relate, while upsetting her mate
a recent bedtime story.

One day when father roused him,
"Cooing" wake up curly head
time for little baby boys
to finish all their broth,
yawning wide, just like Daddy he replied.
Why don't you fuck off?

The 'F' word in this little epos
was used (after much agonising) illustrating
to the "thinking Mum"
why parents should never swear in front of the children

There's another version of this poem for childrens' parties, the 'F' word being mimed, not spoken.

HEROIC TERRORISM?

The things he did rotten
are long since forgotten.
the cries and calls
from shattered malls

Opponents faces blistered
in flaming rubber pyres,
a means of execution
only evil could inspire
death by unspeakable suffering
taunted in agonized throes.
Winnies idea of punishment,
so the story goes.
Nelson being the "nice guy"
just wanted, to cut off their nose.

Do M'Guiness and Gerry Adams.
naively expect, the love and respect,
from the Irish who live in the bogs.
Or reviled in the annals of history.
when they finally pop THEIR clogs?

This is the only critical comment
of a recent event you're liable to hear
but I certainly wouldn't be confident
of an automatic place in Heaven.
If I were him.
And especially his ex Missus.

THERE IS SUCH A THING AS FREE HIGHER EDUCATION

If you can't afford college fees, there are many establishments that will provide an education with free board and lodging, only difference being you don't get any holidays.

Monday morning at Strangeways
wrong side of the turn-keys gate
where new arrivals gather, uncertain of their fate
taunted, laughed at, welcome to "hell"
apprehensive, fidgety, allocated a cell.

One arrogant tearaway,
in and out of long term stay
always at the juvenile courts
for his crimes he has to pay
what little time he spends at home
he's always in the way.

Father is a bully,
life's a constant row,
mother is a pissed up,
substance using cow.

Dependent on weekly handouts, courtesy Nanny State
on the streets abandoned, totally degenerate,
a life of abject squallor, on the local sink estate.
Standing before the Warden, eyes fixed upon the floor
flashing mental images of incarcerations galore.

It started as a ten year old, in and out of bovver
One theft, quickly followed,
by another, and another.
A wealth of criminal knowledge
assures an appetite sated with porridge
and, sure enough, with the passage of time
gets too old for juvenile crime.

Attaining eighteen years of age
guarantees promotion
to the grown-ups' cage.

Sentence to a period, of thirty six months in time
means a free ten term scholarship,
at the Academy of crime.
Like a boarding school pupil
but with motives more sinister
not for him a future as Tory Prime Minister.

His ambition is to join the criminal elite
with honours, in violence thieving, and deceit
unlike the public schoolboy whose tutor is
a well spoken spoken chum.

The prison tutor's English,
is thick with an accent from Brum
adjectives used are expletives,
more Bermigum than plum,

The only thing in common they share
apart results on paper
is the wonderful, long dark twelve hour nights
of dedicated instruction,
on how to make use of one's rectal canal,
from its usual, everyday function.

It didn't do me any harm?

AN UNUSUAL CHRISTMAS PRESENT

Always be nice to the family because as you get older and impatient even your taken for granted loved ones' degrees of affection might drop below frosty.

Don't get out much anymore,
my reputation's a crushing old bore,
a super curmudgeon, king of all grouchers,
family sent me this year,
euthanasia vouchers.

Thought they were having a bit of a laugh
with it being the festive season,
but the bastard's quickly followed them up,
with a one way ticket – to Sweden.

But on booking the flight,
made a terrible gaff,
giving me ironically
the very last laugh.

The ticket plus insurance,
was best part of a grand
had to stump up another five hundred
should've been to Switzerland.

This armistice day poem is an observation slightly tinged with cynicism of how Governments take advantage of the jingoistic nature of their young citizens, turn them into killers for participation in wars disguised as "good against evil", the true motive being the threat to economic growth or restriction of its spread. Without a thought for the future mental anxiety these young warriors will experience, on attaining a deeper thinking maturity.

It's a poem looking at differing points of view from every level of society, the aristocrat terrified at the unthinkable consequences on being vanquished, through to the unwashed have nots, who at the other extreme, would not expect much of a change in circumstance, but on the other hand could possibly benefit, dependent on the reasons for their adversaries campaign, as demonstrated in some modern day conflicts.

ELEVEN. ELEVEN.

"We're here again"
opening wounds, reliving the pain.
Wrinkled ex squaddie proud and tall,
limps past the Cenotaph along Whitehall
involuntary tears run to rest,
darkening colours on be-ribboned chest,
recalling the noise, the confusion, the fright,
the smell of burnt cordite, the blackness of night.

Chanting Bishop commends the bold,
to the fidgeting crowd, wet and cold
"They shan't grow old as we grow old"
Widowed Mum, head bowed on chest,
only Son lost, sixteen years from her breast,
once gentle features, timeworn, stressed
trembling, sobbing, bereft, alone.
Inconsoled on being told,
unlike us, he won't grow old

Royal family on the scene
plump red faced general turns to the Queen
the Hoi Pilloi seem content, to be told
it's great to die young, and not to grow old.
that needless slaughter in the mud
was done for the sake of the greater good.
Can't understand why they never wondered
was it for "quarrelling Royals"
or the Footsie one hundred?

Frail German veteran of ninety years
endures each night, dreams horror filled
with the terrified face, of the youth he killed
locked in his brain, unable to find
some sort of closure, some peace of mind.
Conscience condemns him to live, without joy,
for taking the life, of that poor widow's boy,

Caring wife prays,
for an end to his plight,
the lack of sleep, the dread of night
comforts her husband,
clasping the hand,
that ended a life, in no man's land.

Pitted bones in poppy fields mould
and I'm sure in spite, of what we're told
would prefer to grow old, as we grow old.
Encased in clay concealed from view
for answering the call.
"YOUR COUNTRY NEEDS YOU!"

This Jewel, this England, this Sceptred Isle,
steeped in wealth and noble tradition,
rejected many a volunteer,
stunted by malnutrition.

Unlike the healthy fit and bold
with a ten to one chance not to grow old.
dismissed back to homes damp and cold.
for CERTAIN death without growing old.

No mournful lamentation no gloried recollection,
these wretches could expect.
Unremembered Establishment victims,
of Brittania's shameful neglect.

I find it hard to believe that mature intelligent people can be taken in by some of the so called miracles performed in the new testament. I suppose it's the result of being indoctrinated from a tender age by sinister people in sinister clothes within the awe inspiring circumstance of a massive building which in turn is surrounded by an assortment of dead bodies in various states of decay.
All this I believe is part of an insidious plan to infiltrate young minds with what they would in these modern times describe as harmful unwanted malware, once implanted, difficult and in some cases impossible to remove.

A MODERN DAY MIRACLE

When Jesus got his head in a mess
what they call these days occupational stress
doubting his faith, and what he's about,
went for a walk in the stony without

Roaming the desert confirming his views
God shouted down Son, I've got good and bad news
the bad news is, amongst this grit,
there's nowt to eat but camel shit
what's the good news Dad?
There's tons of it.

Can't understand how with a wave of the hand
changes water to wine, gets cripples to walk
the deaf to hear, the dumb to talk
would venture forth, without drink or crust
and gorge himself on, nowt but locusts.
hard to believe, his miracles credible
when he coudn't turn bugs into something "like edible"

Breaking for lunch, at the gig on the mount
instead of five loaves and a couple of trout
why not locusts and camel pats, to get 'em all fed
easy compared to raising the dead.

But not all those cured by God's only son
were happy, after being done,
because of unthought of anomalies
all but a few starved to death
on losing attendance allowances.

Miracles made, however well meant
don't make for a life, that's full and content
bronchitis, arthritis, lacking virility
difficult breathing, fatigue, immobility

The modern way, for relieving stress
the sleepless nights, financial mess
is to fill out a form at the DSS
little effort, for what it entails
and lo, at the end of a couple of weeks
'tis a miracle, never fails
without any meddling from God and his lad
there's pots of cash in the mail.

Happy folk from Perth to Dover
dance in the streets
their cups runneth over.

Be encouraged to know an aching back
is not these days so tragic
for the turning of pain to financial gain
as Paul Daniels once said:
"NOW *THAT'S* MAGIC!"

RHYMEING TIMES

I've travelled countless millions of miles during my life on this vehicle we call Earth, without getting anywhere beyond where I am now. This repetitive circling seems to be the fundamental principle necessary for the upkeep of boring annuals like Christmas, Wimbledon and Bake Off.
Oh, how much more interesting my life could have been might Earth have taken a straight trajectory now and again? For a welcome departure from the usual spin of things.

Lightning Source UK Ltd.
Milton Keynes UK
UKHW041504010920
369162UK00001B/48

9 781782 224907